# The Mosaik Miracle

How God is Building a New Church for
Refugees, Immigrants, and Nationals

Dr. Stephen Beck

Greater Europe Mission, Monument, Colorado
© 2018 by Greater Europe Mission
All rights reserved. No part of this book may be used or reproduced in any manner
without written permission.
www.GEMission.org

Created in the Unites States of America.

ISBN-13: 978-0-9981864-8-1

This book was originally published in Germany as
*Mission Mosaikkirche: Wie Gemeinden sich für Migranten und Flüchtlinge Öffnen.*
© 2017 Brunnen Verlag GmbH. Gießen, Germany
www.brunnen-verlag.de

# DEDICATION

I dedicate the book in English, as I did in German, to the 24
seminary students who had the courage to launch a church that is
now impacting people in and of many nations, and to all those who
will be inspired to "try the impossible" by their story.

# CONTENTS

# FOREWORD

This book is about a lot of things.

It's about church planting and multiplication, about how a group of students started something in Frankfurt, Germany, that just kept going and growing and multiplying. Looking back, it is clear that the something was a God-thing. Rapid reproduction of churches is a phenomenon that happens all over the world. But the fact that this story happens on the spiritually darkest continent of the world, Europe, where few churches grow, and even fewer multiply, makes the multiplication of a student-run congregation from one to more than 12 churches in six years rather unique.

I want to be upfront and clear with the reader at this point: these 12 congregations are new, fairly small, and even fragile. They have all the usual challenges churches face—chaotic phases, relational messes, the "first-in-first-out syndrome": people who initially are the most enthusiastic to join a church plant can often be the first to leave with bitter accusations toward the church planter for failing to create a church according to their expectations.

The congregations in the Frankfurt-metropolitan region I describe have experienced or are experiencing all of these things. In no way do I wish to elevate any of these churches as the latest success formula for how we "do church" in the 21st century. The uniqueness of the Frankfurt story–which fills the first two chapters of this book–lies merely in the fact that one struggling church plant multiplied itself into 12 congregations within six years, they multiplied in different ways and not just by one method of reproduction, and these congregations joined various denominations while remaining closely tied to one another through the same church DNA. At first, we called it the multi-DNA; eventually, we came to call it the Mosaik-DNA (German for *mosaic*), which I describe in detail in chapter four. The purpose, then, of telling you the unlikely story of a church-planting movement in the Frankfurt-metropolitan region is not to put this particular church on a pedestal. In fact, I will tell you of other churches in this book, which, in other European cities, have experienced a similar thing. This book is a collective testimony that churches become dynamic and grow and multiply when they inject themselves consciously or unconsciously with a Mosaik-DNA.

This brings me to my own experience as a seminary professor and church pastor. This book recounts the biggest adventure I have had in my life. If you had told me in 2011, while the students and I were struggling to keep our fragile experiment of a church plant from imploding, that in a year's time Muslims would walk into our church and into churches all over Europe, ask to become Christians, and be radically transformed by the gospel, I would have given you the address for the nearest clinic that treats people with hallucinatory problems. Never have I experienced the power of God in the gospel and in a gospel community like I have in Frankfurt, Germany. I am compelled to say that what has happened is far beyond ingenious strategy. Foreigners and refugees showing up in our churches and asking, "Who is Jesus?" and "How do I become a Christian?" is not something one can strategize. That is why the motive behind this book is not to create a new network of churches, nor to make a name for anyone or any church, nor to begin an organization known for being highly effective. This is about God doing an unusual thing, about us worshipping him and thanking him for it, about us asking what the special elements in God's unique work are and recognizing these as the DNA of his movement, and intentionally incorporating these elements into everything we do.

This book is also about one of the most formidable challenges Europe has ever faced: the immigration of millions of people who have fled Islamist butchery in their war-torn homelands. Since 2011 distraught and traumatized people have traveled across Middle Eastern roads, African deserts, and Mediterranean waters to Europe. The politicians and the media call it a "refugee crisis." What is not reported, however, is the effect these people have on small, struggling churches (like ours) when they step into Christian communities. The politicians' "crisis" becomes the church's catalyst for change. That is what I will tell you about in this book, especially in chapters three and five through eight. Churches change into a dynamic work of God's Spirit when they open themselves to strangers, foreigners, and radical non-Christians and when they see the immigrant as sent by God. The conversion of foreigners in any church means the renewal of the nationals in that congregation.

This book, therefore, is, in the end, not a call for so-called "refugee churches", nor for churches to merely focus on the latest wave of foreigners coming to our towns and cities. It is a call to the Church to consciously and intentionally do what we should have done many decades ago when we realized our society was becoming multicultural. We should have looked at the waves of immigration far deeper than just the socio-geopolitical level. We should have seen God's hand and heard God's call. The Bible puts it in terms of the "Abrahamic blessing" going to the nations (Genesis 12:1-3) and the consequent manifesto to God's people to have a special heart for the foreigner in their midst (Deuteronomy 10:18-19).

Dietrich Bonhoeffer used the words "church for others" ("Kirche für Andere") in 1944. We today can call it the Mosaic Church. The refugee wave that swept over Europe, and especially over my country, Germany, starting in 2011, is both God's stern reminder and renewed opportunity—maybe the final opportunity we get—to consciously and intentionally open our hearts and our church communities to all the immigrants in our midst we have ignored for so long.

As I give you accounts of churches that have been deeply blessed because they embraced "the Abrahamic blessing", you will read how European national Christians seized the moment and broke out of their monocultural comforts to integrate people of diverse backgrounds, languages, and religions. The current refugee wave has pushed churches to adopt a new normal, which is for the congregational life overall to be driven by the national culture and language while simultaneously and enthusiastically giving the immigrant and immigrant cultures their rightful place of equality, respect, and celebration in the church. It makes for what we will call a mono-multicultural church.

And last but not least, this book is a testimony to the breathtaking changes taking place. As I started writing in early 2016, we were still a small network of 10 churches in the Frankfurt area. Then the opportunities came quickly, and, in many places, new networks grew. In our own region, nine churches were newly planted or joined our network. In Germany, the MissionMosaik movement began, which formed a network of churches from all over Germany and carried the Mosaik-DNA into various organizations. At the same time, contacts with other Europeans were made, and I was invited to speak at conferences in other European nations. What I had planned to fulfill in the Epilogue actually became the most broadly expanding part, so that in fall 2016, I completely rewrote the book, and Frauke Bielefeldt joined me as co-author.

Part 1 describes the history of Mosaik from the initial point of our Mosaik churches (Chapter 1) with their special growth factors (Chapter 2) through the special experience of the flood of refugees (Chapter 3), to the MissionMosaik movement (Chapter 4). Part 2 examines the theological (Chapter 5) and practical (Chapter 6) foundations of the mono-multicultural church and explains what this means for evangelism (Chapter 7), worship services (Chapter 8), church life (Chapter 9), and conversion and baptism (Chapter 10). Finally, I turn to the fears

(Chapter 11) and points of frustration (Chapter 12), which play a special role in mono-multicultural churches.

So then, this book is an invitation to you, dear reader, to seize this special opportunity that God has created in history! The Lord of the nations is calling people of every tongue, tribe, and nation to himself "until the fullness of the Gentiles is come" (Romans 11:25). He has initiated a movement—a wave—in the form of millions of refugees. Ride this wave with us, and, in so doing, jump into your greatest adventure!

And finally, a heads-up and a few acknowledgements. Everything written here depicted the situation in early 2017. Things developed quickly in the final months of writing, during which time we rewrote a number of passages. This book was released in June 2017 and may no longer represent the current situation, whether in the description of the individual Mosaik churches, the status of the MissionMosaik movement, or the socio-political situation. I may need to write the second volume before you have finished reading this one!

I give special thanks to my wife, Susan. She is not only my steady, nearest partner in my ministry, but her quiet, peaceful manner, her eye for detail, and her commitment to me and to the challenging call of God, makes her my backbone in my otherwise turbulent life. She spent many hours with the manuscript I first wrote in English. Thank you, Susan!

Many thanks to Florian Hoenisch for the first German translation and to my colleagues at the Freie Theologische Hochschule Gießen for their many helpful suggestions for the manuscript: Prof. Dr. Armin Baum, Prof. Dr. Ulrike Treusch, Prof. Dr. Christoph Raedel, Dr. Joel White, Dr. Heiko Wenzel, and Ford Munnerlyn. Special thanks also to my colleagues in ministry in many places around the world who read the manuscript and encouraged me to publish it. Thanks, too, to the team at Brunnen Publishing, especially Uwe Bertelmann, who walked with me during this project, and to my editor, Frauke Bielefeldt, who spent many hours working with the puzzle pieces to create the German version of this book. Frau Bielefeldt invested hours in each word and sentence, and at many points improved the quality so much that I decided to include her as co-author.

And then a final thanks to Chancellor Angela Merkel, whose courageous, controversial decision in summer 2015 to allow refugees into Germany made this development possible. This decision has cost her a great deal, but, for me, she remains an example of how a politician can express her Christian faith through love, mercy, and justice.

# 1 THE MOSAIK STORY

## Winds of change blowing across Europe

*"We would have never come up with the idea ourselves to bring people from other cultures into our church."*

**A German Christian, January 2016**

## February 1957

A foreigner in Germany! Not exactly the best prospect for life, given the history of Germany's treatment of foreigners. But that was my lot. At the age of 18 months I was brought to Heidelberg by my American parents. I grew up feeling like a German among Germans, but I wasn't one, and I wasn't treated as one. In my childhood I could not comprehend the animosity I experienced from some Germans—that stern look that bored right through me when the German discovered I was born in New York, or when I would hear a popular scolding that flowed from the lips of Germans with a growl: "Ami, go home!" These were the post-war years of Germany.

Things did not improve when my family moved to Vienna, Austria. In fact, some of my high school teachers slapped me regularly in the face or called me to the front of the class and derided me for being stupid. Only later in life did I learn that my two main professorial antagonists in Austria had served in the Secret Service during World War II.

I returned to the land of my birth in my seventeenth year of life, not sure if I was American, German, or Austrian. Just shy of my eighteenth birthday, I met the girl of my dreams. I married Susan at age 20 and had four children with her. Theology–the study of God and the Scriptures–became my focus, and I studied the Scriptures all the way to a Ph.D. I enjoyed the intellectual depths of theological study, but most of all, I enjoyed serving Jesus by planting churches and pastoring the churches I planted. First, Susan and I planted a church in a town of 12,000 in the USA, then in the megacity, Toronto, Canada. We became Canadian citizens so Germans would never again say to me, "Ami, go home!"

Actually, I did not want to return to Germany. There were simply too many bad memories of critically minded people who lacked any sense of humor, scolded me for things that were none of their business, or slapped me around in school when my best was not good enough. Obviously, the chorus "Ami, go home!" had scarred me. You can imagine the internal storm that began to rage in my soul when an email from Germany in 2002 essentially read: "Ami, come over and help us!" It was an invitation from the Freie Theologische Hochschule (FTH) in Giessen (the Giessen School of Theology) to teach practical theology. I was asked to teach everything I knew about serving Jesus in and through the church, including a course on how to start new churches. The fight between the hidden scars and the call of God on my life made for a storm in my soul and in my family that raged for three years. In September 2005, Susan and I gave in and moved to Germany.

The "Ami" came home!

## January 31, 2011

We held our first gathering. Twenty-four students of the FTH Giessen[1] declared themselves ready to try an experiment in Frankfurt. We called it "Church for all Nations." I saw it as the "Church for Others"—or at least as my application of what Dietrich Bonhoeffer had called for, when in 1944 he argued against the Church's status quo and for a so-called "Kirche für Andere" (Church for others)[2].

In my lectures at the seminary in Germany, I insisted that a church that functions monoculturally, i.e., functions circularly around one culture group, is out of step with the ever-growing diversity within society. The way to implement Bonhoeffer's biblical concept of Church for Others was for the Church to respond to the waves of immigration since the end of WWII. I would take the students into the Scriptures and show them the centrality of the stranger in God's plan of salvation. The obedient Church of Jesus does not protect itself from strangers but opens its doors to them. As strangers from everywhere had increasingly turned Germany's metro regions into global villages, the Church's only Jesus-like response would be to become the Church for Others. In an increasingly multicultural society, the Church does not have the option to remain monocultural.

Strictly speaking, Church for all Nations was not supposed to be a multicultural church. It was supposed to be comprised of Germans, on one hand, and of all other nations, such as Turks, Greeks, Serbs, Jews, and Koreans, on the other hand. I did not know what to call it. The word "multicultural" did not fit, so I called it the "50/50 model". In other words, we envisioned a church comprised in part of German nationals and in part of nationalities that had arrived in Germany in the three major immigration waves since WWII. Intercultural reconciliation through the power of the gospel was to be the most prominent of our core values[3].

Our DNA factors, from which we drew our core values and strategies, were "multicultural," "multi-lingual," "multi-site," "multi-networked," and "multiplicational". We joked about being a multi-everything church.

Our church plant was to function as a training ground for the students.

They were supposed to experience practically what they learned in my classes, then multiply it throughout the Frankfurt-RheinMain metro region. We planned to plant 10 congregations by 2025: four in Frankfurt, one in Giessen, one somewhere between Giessen and Frankfurt, one in Wiesbaden, one in Offenbach, one in Mainz, and one in Darmstadt. Although I loved Frankfurt for its prominence and influence, I especially cherished the thought of one of my students planting a Church for all Nations in Darmstadt. Why? That was where I spent my early years in life, and where people would say to me, "Ami, go home!" I resolved in 2011 that I would not return home until the church in Darmstadt was planted.

*We also decided—and people really thought this was a curious thing— that every one of these congregations would be allowed to decide not only what its name would be but to which denomination it would belong. What would connect us as a network of churches was the same DNA, what we would later come to call the Mosaik-DNA (Chapter 3). We believed we could serve the denominations of our country, if, with each new church, we could tell the denominations in Germany: "Whoever would like to adopt this church plant as its own can have it, so long as the planter may operate within the principles of church planting he has learned and the biblical theology he holds to, and the denomination contributes at least a third of his salary to the work."

We had prayed a lot together, and we were dreamers. Of course, by most people's assessment, we were not only dreamers–we were crazy. But we thought big, because we believed it was time for a new paradigm, a new normal for the Church. With great eagerness we approached our first meeting in Frankfurt on January 31, 2011. Many people of German descent as well as of different nationalities had indicated they would come.

They didn't! Other than those of us from the FTH in Giessen and a few student friends from the University of Giessen, only six people from Frankfurt showed up. Every church plant must be started with the possibility of failing. Risk is a normal element in church planting, just like planting many seeds in the ground does not guarantee that each seed will blossom into a flower. But that meeting on a cold winter afternoon in Frankfurt made the risk of failure clearer to me than I had anticipated. My anxiety was only heightened by the next several meetings we held in a building that belonged to the Protestant state church. The "Frankfurters" were not increasing. Just the opposite. The situation became especially critical for us when the state church pastor, who had promised us the use of the most prominent church building in Frankfurt, discovered that we were evangelical in theology. From one day to the next, he threw us out and wanted no more association with our group. Just like that, we were a homeless church plant.

I honestly don't know what kept us going. Was it fear of failing at the very thing I taught students in class? Was it faith and confidence that we had not mistaken God's calling to plant this particular kind of church? Was it the students and their undying enthusiasm for starting something new? Was it a little bit of everything? I don't know. I do know that for a year and a half we bounced along from one week to the next, and we often drove home from meetings discouraged.

In retrospect, we see now that God had something "crazier" in mind than what we had dreamed. The real craziness was about to begin.

## October 2012

October 31, Reformation Sunday. Nobody in Church for all Nations could have foreseen that this Sunday in 2012 would move the tiny church plant in a new direction. Three things came together on the 495th anniversary of the Reformation:

First of all, against all natural wisdom and after prolonged discussions with two existing church groups, I decided to bring them in under our "church-planting roof". Both congregations were small and had started to question whether or not they could survive. On the weekend of

Reformation Sunday, we celebrated the merger of the three groups. From this point on, we started calling this concept of church "MosaikChurch" (Mosaikkirche)[4]. We had not originally thought of multiplication this way, but I concluded it was an effective way to train the students for further multiplication. I divided the group of students between the three congregations, which met for worship in different locations at different times. This way, all students were able to participate in the development of a church plant through providing the congregations with leadership, preaching, evangelistic groups, and pastoral care. I gave oversight and mentoring to all three congregations. As creative as this appeared in the German context, it was risky. We were no longer one fragile church plant, we were three. Failure would not merely affect 40 people but 100.

The second contributing growth factor was an American missionary. Political correctness in 2012 no longer allowed Germans to say, "Ami, go home!" The fact of the matter was that we were so desperate, nobody even thought about using the old slur. This woman had raised all her own financial support in order to serve full time in our three congregations. She was a special gift to us. Mature, warm-hearted, and loving, eager to lead people to faith in Jesus and to disciple people new in the faith, Karen Smith[5] immediately became a "mother" figure to all the young people and to the first few refugees that arrived.

The matter with the refugees became the third catalytic development on October 31, 2012: A young Afghan man named Raifa[6] entered the worship service that Sunday. It did not matter to him that there were only a few people in the worship service. What he immediately found attractive was the kindness of the people, especially Karen Smith. Raifa had recently converted from Islam to following Jesus. Karen was delighted to invest in the ex-Muslim and disciple him in his new life. The Persian man was also delighted to see the translation equipment that was set up but still unused. For Raifa that meant that if he could learn German quickly, he could invite other Afghans from the refugee center into this church community and translate for them into Farsi. His countrymen would be able to hear the gospel of Jesus.

The next week Raifa brought another Afghan to the worship service. The week after that another one. Every week he brought more of his countrymen. Karen made sure Persian Bibles were available. Then— with the help of another American—she organized German lessons for the refugees and called it Café Hope.[7] Word spread that a worship service in Frankfurt offered simultaneous translation. Some Iranians who lived a two-hour train ride away heard that they could learn in their own language who Jesus is, and began to make the weekly train ride to the worship services. To honor their long trip and efforts, Karen began to hold Persian Bible classes after the worship services. With Raifa rapidly growing in German language skills, the post-service group became a tool to disciple Raifa in his knowledge of Scripture and, at the same time, bring Muslims to Christ. The first Muslims gave Jesus their lives and were baptized. It created a tremendous dynamic in the congregation. Germans were swept up in the movement of the Spirit and also let themselves be baptized into following Jesus in faith.

It began to dawn on us that God had called us to plant a German church, not merely for the people who had come in the first three immigration waves, but for the people he was sending as the fourth wave. More and more we realized that three congregations—one in Frankfurt-North (the original Church for all Nations), one in Frankfurt-Northeast, and one in the Frankfurt suburb of Oberursel—were born and growing with the same Mosaik-DNA, because God had created a wave he wanted us to ride.

## January 2015

A few of the original 24 students decided the worship services were not enough; they wanted community with each other during the week, a small group in Giessen (we called our small groups "house churches"), in which they could celebrate what God had begun in their church plant and in which they could pray intensely for more. At first, six students met on a Wednesday evening. Their lives and witness were so powerful that within six months the group increased to 30 students. It was time to start another congregation.

On January 22, 2015, almost four years after launching the first church plant, the fourth Mosaik congregation held its first worship service in a rented movie theater: Mosaik-Giessen. More than 100 people attended that first service, including many non-Christians and foreigners. One of them was Jahni. He had heard about Jesus for the first time in his life shortly before leaving his country a few months earlier. Jahni did not know German, but God knew that Jahni needed the gospel. Karen Smith and several others from Mosaik in Frankfurt-North had driven the 60 kilometers to help celebrate the multiplication of Mosaik. When shortly before the sermon the worship leader asked if anyone needed English translation, Jahni raised his hand. He knew English. Karen immediately left her seat and sat down next to the young man and translated the sermon for him.

Nobody could know that with the launch of this church plant God would forever change Jahni's life. As circumstances would have it, authorities moved the refugee to another city shortly after the opening service. But Jahni was desperate to know God. He searched the internet for the name of the church and its closest congregation. Then he made the hour-long train ride to the worship service of Frankfurt-North, as the original Church for all Nations was the closest Mosaik location. There he made a surprising discovery: Right in front of him stood the woman who had translated the sermon in Giessen for him a few months earlier, Karen Smith! God's hand was guiding every step of Jahni's journey.

In the summer of 2015, Jahni's life was turned upside down: He announced to his family that he was going to follow Jesus as his Savior and Lord. His parents were furious. Not long after "outing" himself as a Christian, the police appeared at his door step and shipped the illegal refugee back to his homeland. He went willingly and peacefully. He knew the purpose for his brief stay in Germany. In fact, he now knew the purpose of his life. It was Jesus!

What our students and Susan and I had begun as an experiment, now had developed into four congregations with a Mosaik-DNA. God was just getting started!

## May 2015, "Little Istanbul", Offenbach, Germany

Offenbach is a city many prefer to avoid. A high crime rate combined with a high immigrant ratio and a strong Salafisten movement, this place is not desirable to young, well-educated German families. That is why Lionel and Naemi Bendobal moved there with their little boy in May 2015. The couple had been part of the original 24 students who had dreamed the dream of "Church for Others". They could not think of any better place to extend the open arms of Jesus to "others" than in Offenbach.

Klaus and Debora[8] are two ordinary Germans who grew up in an ordinary small town in an ordinary church. Toward the end of their Bible school education, they heard about Lionel, the young Cameroonian, who had been part of Church for all Nations and now was planting a congregation in Offenbach that would belong to Klaus and Debora's denomination. They were immediately taken with the vision and DNA of the new church plant. They felt great respect for the young Bendobal family to move into a troubled city. So, they decided to move to Offenbach and commit themselves to God's kingdom work through the next church plant with the Mosaik-DNA.

But before they did that, they participated in a Mosaik "family festival"– the first gathering of the various church plants and their members. The couple speaks today of the enthusiasm they felt when they arrived at the festival of a small multiplication movement of which they had heard so much. Looking back several months later, Klaus commented:

"Our enthusiasm quickly turned to irritation. We walked into the large room where we were to meet and immediately noticed that most of the people were very different than us. There were people of 26 different nations there. In fact, we at first did not see many white people. Then a group of 30 Iranians walked in—complete strangers to all of us—and they simply plopped themselves into the middle of the room and waited for the food to be served. Even an atheist from Israel was there. We found ourselves in the middle of chaos as we heard Spanish, English, Arabic, Farsi, German, and other languages being spoken simultaneously. When Stephen Beck got up to speak, the translators in the back of the room were louder than he was in the front. We felt completely overwhelmed. The most irritating thing to us was that most of the people appeared to be enjoying this mess. It just did not meet our expectations of a quiet and orderly gathering."

Klaus and Debora's spinning heads went into overdrive when I started explaining MosaikChurch with words like "We are not monocultural; we are not multicultural; we are mono-multicultural", or "the macro level" and the "micro level". They wondered how many other M-words I would come up with to confuse the world. Then I started talking about the vision of transporting this chaos to other European countries and as far as Tel Aviv, Israel. "Why Tel Aviv?" Klaus whispered to Debora with sarcasm. "Everybody else talks about Jerusalem." The couple was alarmed: What had they agreed to join? How was this philosophy of ministry compatible with that of their denomination? Did they want to belong to something that thinks outside of their box? These and other questions accompanied the couple to their home later that day.

The same questions accompanied Klaus and Debora to the first meetings in Offenbach with people interested in the church plant. There were many conversations with others, many presentations from Lionel, and always these ridiculous M-words! After four months, Klaus and Debora found themselves in a private conversation with Lionel and Naemi, who asked them how they were feeling about the city they had moved to and the church plant they were going to work in. The German pair relayed the misgivings with which they had left the "family festival" several months earlier. This is Klaus' account of what he said:

> "Today we see things a little differently than four months ago. We love our denomination, but we realize that ultimately church planting is not about planting a denominational church that upholds the structure and traditions we have come to appreciate. It's about belonging to a denomination without thinking about how we fit into our denomination. It's about being uncompromised in our biblical theology while having what Lionel calls a mosaic-mentality about the church, a heart for the nations and for the unconverted, with which we approach different cultures, different educational levels, different languages and skin colors with a friendly and welcoming heart. The difference between my old church and the new one we are planting is that I don't see the 'others' as people our church will never touch but as the people we are meant to touch. I have to take the time to get to know them, go where they are, spend time with them, understand their way of life, and even learn from them. We are not talking about a head-to-head approach; it is heart-to-heart. It is opening our hearts to others. It is humbling ourselves before others, hearing others, learning from others, and serving others. It's about becoming a church for others."

Debora jumped in at that point and continued:

> "I think that is the crux for me. We don't ask anymore how the others fit into our denominational structures, but the other way around: how does our denomination fit into the culture of the people we are trying to reach? The people don't serve our denomination; our denomination serves the people."

Lionel had restrained himself. But now he could not hold back anymore and burst out with a loud, African "Hallelujah!"

The start team of the Offenbach church worked hard at networking, doing surveys, getting into people's homes, and learning about their lives and needs. Each start team member had the responsibility to build up his or her network of non-Christian friends. And when it was time for the first test-worship service, 62 people were present: 12 were the start-team; 50 were unchurched. The same number came to the second test-worship service. The church called itself Kirche am Start (Church in the beginning), the fifth intentional church plant with a Mosaik-DNA.

## March 2016 in an Undesirable Frankfurt Neighborhood

Nordweststadt was built in the 1960s for the express purpose of placing new immigrants there. New arrivals from non-German descent and culture were not to move into the already crowded city center of Frankfurt; they were to move to Nordweststadt on the outskirts of the city. Fifty years later this part of Frankfurt is known to insiders as a place of crime, high suicide rate, and Muslims. Seventy percent of the population is immigrant. The isolation of this part of the city expresses itself in the complete absence of any restaurant. There is no place to meet around good food. For the 18,000 people living there, there is not a single evangelical church.

Jason is one of the original 24 students who started Church for all Nations. When he first heard of Nordweststadt, his heart broke. A year after he married Steffi, he moved to this "eye of the tiger". Jason and Steffi are Germans who know how it feels to be outsiders: he grew up in Thailand; Steffi in Bangladesh. Now it was the German couple's turn to be the host and to welcome the stranger into their midst. They moved to the top floor of one of the many high rises and into the midst of people where everybody is nobody. "In fact," explains Jason, "this is the part of Frankfurt The Beatles must have written their song about: 'He's a real nowhere man, living in his nowhere land, making all his nowhere plans for nobody.'"

Their goal was to plant an evangelical congregation in this district. There was formerly a small church in this neighborhood. A German pastor, Bernd Oettinghaus, and his family had planted a congregation in this neighborhood in the 1990s. For 15 years his church plant had slowly blossomed with growth. But under Bernd's successor, the work collapsed quickly, and the spiritual lights in this city district went out. Ever since then, Bernd and two of his former parishioners, including pediatrician Klaus Behr[9], prayed every Wednesday morning at 6:30 a.m. at the location of the former church. They prayed that someday the gospel would resound in that building again. They vowed to keep praying until the prayer was answered, and they planted a tree as a sign of their covenant with the head of the church.

But God seemed to have gone on holiday: a developer purchased the building with the intent of tearing it down and building a high rise. The three men remained undaunted in their Wednesday morning prayer. Then the developer went bankrupt and sold to another developer. This one had the same intention as the first developer. He also had the same result of bankruptcy. And, believe it or not, a third developer purchased the former church site in order to turn it into a high rise. But he, too, went bankrupt. God obviously had not gone on vacation. He was present and involved in the plans for this building.

In 2013 the city decided to take ownership of the building and turn it into a community center. Hundreds of thousands of Euros were invested to refurbish the building. An urban planning commission was to decide which organizations were allowed to move into the edifice and offer this urban "no-man's-land" life-enriching activities and services. Jason and Steffi applied to the commission and asked that the young couple's future church plant be allowed to move into the building. The local mosque also put in a request, offering a substantial amount of money to rent the large hall. All applications went to the mayor. She decided that an evangelical church be granted permission to operate in the new community center.

*Years of Wednesday morning prayers had been answered by God.*

But God had decided to take the process even higher than any of us had imagined. There where the little covenant tree stood, the city decided to respond to the tidal wave of refugees by building a refugee center. And more, the kindergarten leader in the building next to the refurbished community center and the refugee center under construction heard about the new initiative with the Mosaik-DNA. She invited Jason to begin a German class in her kindergarten for the parents of the children. Most of them did not know German.

Jason began to network with everything that moved. He contacted stores, clubs, work places, people on the street, in the parks, in the apartment buildings, in a local youth organization, and leaders of the mosque. Jason and Steffi held a Christmas Eve party in their apartment for residents of Nordweststadt. They began a prayer group. Any way they could offer community to the lonely and isolated, they did.

Their best friends, Kevin and Christina, who also were part of the original student group that started Mosaik, moved in 2016 into the same high rise as Jason and Steffi. Jason's role was to be the evangelist-pastor, the gatherer, the networker. Kevin's role as "second pastor" was that of a pastoral caretaker. In February 2016, the two couples held a brunch worship service and only seven people came. But when they repeated the event in March 2016, 25 people came: Germans, Argentinians, Spaniards, El Salvadorians, Iranians, Syrians, Russians, Chinese, Japanese, Turks, and a woman from Sierra Leone. In this part of the city, it looked like the church was going to reach immigrants from the migration wave of the 1980s.

With the birth of the sixth congregation in fewer than five years, we were becoming certain that God had swept us up into something extraordinary for a European country. This church plant gave itself the name Kirche für Nordwest (Church for Northwest), because it envisioned that it would multiply itself into several congregations to the northwest of Frankfurt-Northwest. Multiplication is a significant part of the Mosaik-DNA.

# November 2015 in Central Frankfurt

Kathi opened her eyes, even though praying with one's eyes closed was the normal custom of the group. She was in a restaurant with her church planting start team. It was a Pakistani restaurant owned by a Muslim man—an unusual place for a church plant to meet for prayer!

Five years earlier she had been part of the FTH Giessen student group that in January 2011 had held its first meeting in Frankfurt. Five years later she had moved to Frankfurt. The Pakistani restaurant was located across the street from her apartment. She had walked into the small place to thank the owner for giving her roommate a job. The Muslim owner, in turn, apologized that he was not able to give Kathi's roommate a full-time job. Business had been bad, the worst in five years. Kathi asked if she could lay hands on the man and pray to God to bless him and his business. He made sure she knew he was Muslim. She was willing to pray for God's blessing anyway. And so she did!

A week later she returned to the restaurant for a quick bite to eat. When the owner saw her, he excitedly went to her and reported that in the past week business had been the best in five years. Kathi responded with delight and offered to pray again. Seven days later she was back. The owner announced: "Your prayers have great power. My business was the best ever this past week, even better than the week before. You must have a special connection to God! Please keep praying for my business, and I will give you free lunch every day you come here. And if your church needs a place to meet, you can use my restaurant. I will even close my business for the times you need it for your church."

That is how the start team ended up in the Pakistani restaurant for prayer five weeks after Kathi's first encounter with the owner. The group was praying intensely when loud and happy conversation on the other side of the large restaurant window caused Kathi to open her eyes. Out on the sidewalk a group of Africans had gathered. The 26-year-old German grabbed her jacket and went outside where 20 Somalis and Eritreans, all Muslims, loudly chattered with each other. The tall, beautiful German interrupted the little community party: "Hi, I am Kathi, and I am the new pastor for this neighborhood. I am so glad to meet you."

The group was immediately attentive. "What is a pastor?" one of the men asked. Kathi told the group that she herself had just recently moved to this part of the city and hoped these Africans could help her learn some things about the streets and the people who lived there.

That was a key moment! The African group took this bright girl into their circle. They started to talk about what it was like to live in the neighborhood. But they also wanted to know what a pastor does, why someone with a master's degree would choose a part of the city notorious for poverty, drugs, prostitution, and immigrant tensions. Soon the Germans from the prayer group came out on the sidewalk and joined their fearless leader. Several more Somalis and Eritreans walked by, stopped, listened, and then joined the group.

Kathi took the conversation deeper. When she felt they had laughed a few times and established some mutual trust, she suggested that everybody explain, from his or her religious perspective, how (if at all) they had experienced God. Several Muslims shared. The exchange became lively and emotional.

Then one of the Africans asked: "What about you Christians? How have you experienced God?"

A young Syrian from the start team, a man who had turned from Islam to Jesus just a few weeks earlier, began to share. Then another person in the start team shared, this time a woman. Everybody listened respectfully.

"How can we Germans be of service to you?" Kathi suddenly asked. That question brought everybody up short. None of the immigrants had expected such an offer from a German. When the silence became uncomfortable, Kathi made a daring suggestion: "Would you all like to meet next week at the same time right here again, and we will continue our friendship?" Everybody enthusiastically agreed.

A week later it was raining. Kathi stood in the downpour and waited. One by one, half the African group came back to the place of meeting. The church planter suggested that due to the inclement weather they all go up to her apartment across the street. For the next several hours, Kathi's apartment was filled with the good aromas of cooking, laughter, and tearful retelling of sad childhoods, civil war, starvation, killings, and horrible crossings from Africa to Europe. Finally, Kathi repeated the question she had asked a week earlier: "How can we Germans be of service to you?"

One woman whispered: "It is good what you are doing right now." A man added: "We need German classes, especially our wives."

Two weeks later, German classes began. Eventually the group of people learning German reached 30. Kathi organized other events that brought the first contacts of the church plant together. Friendships developed. On Easter morning, an Easter service was conducted for the neighborhood...in the Pakistani restaurant, of course. Thirty-two people came, half of them Muslims.

The seventh congregation since birthing Church for all Nations added yet another denominational affiliation to God's little movement. What bonded all seven church plants together was the Mosaik-DNA.

## December 2015 in a Village Outside of Giessen

Pastor Christian Sewerin was dissatisfied not only with his ingrown church and ministry, he was especially discontent with his spiritual life. Somehow over time God had become boring, as if the relationship were merely routine. Christian sensed it was not much different for the members of his congregation. Christianity had become about as static and unexciting as life in the little village in which he lived with his wife, Damaris, and their four children.

At a conference in Basel, Switzerland, to which all pastors of his denomination were expected to come, Christian and I met in November 2015. I was one of two speakers. The 40-year-old pastor heard my presentations about the Church: how the Church is meant to be like a mosaic, mono-multicultural, macro-, micro-, etc. Not everyone was motivated, I'm sure, but for him, the conference became a special encounter with God, perhaps similar to the encounter Jacob had when he met God at the brook of Jabbok (Gen. 32:23-33). Jacob had to wrestle with God all night. For Christian, the conference in Basel became a wrestling match with God. He prayed:

> God, I want your blessing, your very special anointing. I am so tired of living the no-risk, no-change lifestyle. I want to do something new for you. But, first, I myself need to be renewed. I don't even know what that means. I just know my life should amount to more than pastoring a comfortable congregation that hopes nothing ever changes so nothing disturbs its sleep.

That prayer took root deeply in Christian's heart. For weeks it would not let him go. Should he plant a new church? He had heard a lot about church planting from the French speaker, Daniel Liechti, and from me at the conference in Basel. But Christian did not see himself as a church planter. He was more of a shepherd who knows how to care for existing congregations. Added to that, he had a wife and four young children. This was not the time to open himself up to such a high-risk job like planting a new church—not as a responsible German husband and father.

But the night of wrestling with God--or was it God wrestling with Christian—did not end. Resigned to the thought that God wanted to send him limping like Jacob into the future, Christian sent an email to the board chairman of his congregation, to four pastors of churches in the area, to the regional superintendent of his denomination, and to me. We were all invited to his home. Damaris joined us at the table, too. She was interested and curious but skeptical that the other pastors at the table would be receptive to her husband's idea. I, for one, had no idea what that idea might be.

Christian opened in prayer then explained to us all why we were there: he did not think himself qualified to plant a new church, but if someone else would do it, he would be prepared to help. That way he would not need to leave his congregation. He wondered if a few people from each of the congregations could come together and create a start team for a new church. They would not need to leave their own congregations. On Sundays they could be in their own worship services, but during the week, they would help out in the start team. Everything they learned in the start team and the spiritual refreshment they would receive, they would take back to their congregations. Christian wanted to know if the four other pastors would join him in a cooperative church planting venture. At the appropriate time, they would all look for a church planter to take the new congregation forward.

I was totally surprised. A pastor of one denomination asked the pastors of other denominations if their congregations would join in a collaborative effort. "But which denomination will this new church belong to?" I asked.

Christian exploded: "It does not matter! We can decide that later, but for now I don't care. All we need to care about is giving this village a church that has a heart for the unsaved."

I wondered how Christian's superintendent felt about his "disloyal" employee, so I asked more concretely: "You belong to the state church. What if the group decides to join the Pentecostal church?" I could not believe my ears when the superintendent blurted, "That does not matter! So long as this village has a church in which people can encounter Jesus Christ, it does not matter what denomination it is. We want to stand behind it."

It was a most unusual conversation! What was equally unusual is that none of the four other pastors felt threatened by the thought. Precisely the opposite: everybody was interested. I asked if there was a refugee center in the area. "Right here in our town," Damaris chimed in. "Then you have an immediate mission field, around which the start team could orient itself," I said.

This thought hit Damaris like a lightning bolt. Christian's wife, who herself had become dissatisfied with her routine walk with God, said she had just met an Afghan in the refugee center. This man was a Christian and knew English, and that is why he could converse with Damaris.

"There we go!" I said. "Why don't you go back to the Afghan, ask him to invite everybody in the refugee center to a party? Then organize a great evening for the people, maybe a big banquet of sorts." I found it easy to suggest this, since I knew I would not be cooking.

At the conclusion of the evening the group decided to meet after the new year to share their ideas, pray, and plan. But before we all left, Damaris wanted us all to know something: "I came to this evening with a great deal of skepticism. But the idea that I could move into the lives of all those Muslims and strangers in the refugee home...wow! I feel suddenly excited. Thank you all for being such a motivation to me!" We would all learn in the coming weeks that God met with Damaris in a special way that evening.

Three weeks later was Christmas Eve 2015. Twenty Afghans from the refugee center came to the Christmas Eve service in Christian's village church. Nobody in the congregation knew what they should do with these Middle Easterners who did not speak their language. Nobody could remember ever having seen a non-German in the worship service. Now there suddenly were 20 Afghans. Muslims. Persian women with head coverings. The worship service, which was traditionally staid, grew chaotic while Christian pondered how he was going to communicate to people whose language he did not speak. He ended up speaking in German, and a young student stood beside him and translated each sentence into English. The Afghan Christian, who sat in the middle of the Persian group, translated loudly into Farsi for his people. The sermon took three times as long as normal. Some of the Germans minded the slow pace. Christian didn't care. All he could think was that for the first time in his life, he was sharing God's Word with 20 Muslims.

After the service Damaris invited all the Afghans to a Christmas feast. The Germans in the congregation had their own family plans, the same ones they had every year. But, in the Sewerin home, there was a celebration—a loud one! Damaris says it was the best Christmas she had ever experienced.

On the way back to the refugee center, Christian asked the English-speaking Afghan if he could imagine helping Christian start a church in which these and other Afghans in the refugee center could regularly enjoy worship services and come to know Jesus Christ. A smile spread across the Afghan's face.

Several weeks later, two things happened in the village simultaneously: Christian and Damaris commenced German lessons for the refugees. They wanted to meet these dear people in their felt need. They wanted to develop a relationship with these strangers who had been placed in their village. Second—and at the same time—15 Germans met on a Wednesday evening as a start team. The pastors had done it! They had actually encouraged their members to consider working with members of other churches to form a start team and work toward planting a new church. Each of the pastors who had sat at the Sewerins' table weeks before Christmas had urged their congregations to envision a new congregation in the area in which people of all possible backgrounds and religions could find Jesus and receive God's salvation.

Not every believer was happy. In fact, in Christian's own congregation, some people were upset with their pastor, because he was asking them to help start a church that would become a competition to their own church. But something remarkable was happening in these pastors: the feeling of having to hang on to their members had dissolved in a passion to expand the kingdom of God. What had also dissolved was the thought that a church plant is some kind of competition to an existing church.

The next offspring of the original Church for all Nations was conceived, this time in a small village, and this time by someone who was not part of the original group of 24 students. The Mosaik-DNA was spreading.

> *"What you call a mono-multicultural church is what is happening here! The first congregation was planted 40 years ago by immigrants from Russia. There are 30 nationalities in the congregation. About 10 years ago, we started to offer a worship service in Farsi. That work started with six visitors and one couple that functioned as leaders. It grew slowly and consistently to about 160 Persians. Then it started making great leaps. We now count between 350 to 450 visitors to that worship service, and every Sunday Iranians and Afghans are converting to Jesus."*

> **Jakob Goerzen, Pastor of the Protestant Freechurch**
> **Cologne, Germany, 2016**

## January 2016

Simon is different, at least different than a classical church planter. He is quiet and introverted. He does not have a lot of charisma and does not attract attention. What did attract my attention, however, was when he stood up in our preaching class at the seminary and started to preach. He was strong, to the point, and his voice expressed an inner confidence. Consequently, I invited the young man to join the movement of church plants. Immediately it became obvious how Simon quietly moves alongside people in difficult straits and expresses compassion. The natural place for Simon to serve was Café Hope in our first church plant. But when he heard that Jason and Steffi had begun a Café Hope in Nordweststadt, he joined that group as well. Here was a young man with a broken heart for the brokenhearted.

One evening, an unprecedented number of immigrants appeared in

Café Hope in our first church plant (Church for all Nations). Karen Smith and I had the idea that these immigrants should have the opportunity not only to learn German, but to learn German and to learn about the God of the Bible at the same time. It could happen in a Sunday morning community with brunch, joyful singing, Bible lessons in German, language instruction, discussions about the identity of Jesus, and teaching on how to pray to him and through him.

The idea captured Simon's heart. Along with Mira, one of the 24 students who had started the first congregation five years earlier, Simon launched the experiment. A few other students of the FTH joined in. It took a few months before the group had any kind of settled attendance. But even on the Sundays when only three or four guests came, there was a clear awareness of God's presence in the group as well as surprise over the spiritual hunger guests showed regarding the Bible stories. The group steadily grew and included two Syrian Muslim men, whose families were left behind in Damascus; a Syrian-Palestinian woman and her children; a Buddhist woman and her children; Hindu children from the neighborhood; an Eritrean woman; an Albanian woman; a Mexican man; the German students; my wife, Susan; and Karen. The students, Susan, and Karen prepared the brunch each Sunday morning and led the adult group and the children's program. We discovered that the foreigners came because they felt threatened by the larger crowd that met in the classic Mosaik worship service or intimidated by the fast-moving sermon they could not understand.

There is a lot of pastoral care that happens in the Sunday morning brunch gathering. An Albanian woman who comes out of deep poverty and a low level of education found German extremely difficult to learn. One morning one of the team workers figured out that the woman's one-year-old daughter has Down's Syndrome and had been in and out of the hospital with a fever for months. That worker immediately laid her arm around the mother and prayed for the daughter. The immigrant woman began to sob. She wept and wept. There was no way she could understand the content of the prayer, but that did not matter. She was in the presence of God, and she felt that. Her sorrows were poured out on the Almighty in the form of tears.

I decided the form of church that was developing could best fit with Fresh Expressions of Church, a movement of creative, non-traditional forms of church community that started in England at the beginning of the 21st century (see next chapter). In Germany we have simply called it "Fresh-X". What characterizes Fresh-X churches are the very same core values that make up Mosaik churches. Like Mosaik, Fresh-X churches are missional, contextual, life-changing communities of people whose lives have been impacted by the gospel of Jesus. These are different forms of community, worship, and teaching from the other Mosaik church starts in Frankfurt-RheinMain, but the same DNA.

With this Fresh-X church, the ninth Mosaik church plant under the leadership of a 23-year-old student, we felt like we had moved into a new frontier. In fact, it opened our thinking to starting new church communities in Germany much faster than ever before. We only needed to let ourselves be open to the natural context, in this case, the immigrants who suddenly were coming into the country. The refugee crisis provided many of these natural contexts.

## God's "Wave"

In this refugee crisis, the public sees mainly tragedies and political chaos. Many people in Europe see the refugees as a personal threat. Politicians build fences and walls to stem the tide. But when we look through the fog of fear, in which so many people are walking, we see a mighty wave—not only a wave of refugees, but a wave of the gospel and God's grace that has washed over nations, just like God promised in the Scriptures: "...a partial hardening has come upon Israel, until the fullness of the Gentiles has come in. And then all Israel will be saved" (Romans 11:25-26).

When churches open their hearts to refugees and immigrants, they become a part of God's present work of bringing in the fullness of the Gentiles. The result will be a spiritual breakthrough. That is the theme of this book, and I will give you many examples that underscore this thesis. As you read on allow yourself to be drawn into this wave of God.

# 2 HOW COULD IT GROW SO FAST?

*"Our prayer for the people of the world is the best gift that we can give the world."*

**Simon Grunwald (Mosaik Fresh-X)**

Much has happened. As I've been writing this book, additional Mosaik churches are developing. The current nine churches cover an area roughly 100 kilometers long[10] and have a total of about 450 members, a quarter of whom are new converts. How is it possible that the original initiative, Church for all Nations, was able to multiply itself so quickly within five years?

Before I turn to the analysis, I want to emphasize that we do not put a high value on the size of the congregation or the number of worship service visitors. A group of 20 people is just as effective as a group of 100, when non-Christians (nationals, immigrants and refugees) come into the church community and decide to follow Jesus, and when there is a strong emphasis on discipleship and spiritual growth.

So, it's not about having the most people in the church congregation, but rather reaching people outside of the church in their current life situations and desires. Instead of asking how many people are attending worship services, I'm more interested in knowing how many people without a relationship to Jesus are being touched by the church planting project at any given time.

As well, it relieves a great burden on the church planter when he knows that he doesn't have to deliver a certain number of people. "Success" is demonstrated through the church planter's faithfulness as pastor and evangelist. Each location has its own history; each situation is different. Sometimes the ground is frozen solid, while in other locations the ground is already starting to thaw and an openness for God's work is growing.

None of our congregations see themselves as the ideal church or as a model church. They all have to struggle with similar difficulties and challenges, just as churches around the world, for example, with the high turnover in a city context. And just like in other situations, in our Mosaik churches, people become dissatisfied and leave. However, the multiplication over the last five years has been quite fast and, in some ways, unique. In analyzing this development in the Rhein-Main area, there are several factors that have contributed to this growth.

## Openness to a Variety of Models

As the overview in Chapter 1 has shown, the Mosaik churches are examples of various models of church planting. Some resulted from a solo pioneer moving to a location and gathering people from that location for the start team, while others brought the start team with them to the location. Others had a team already on location (to distinguish this from the start team, we'll call this the "core team"), that already had been meeting for some time as a community and then joined the Mosaik Church and called a person from their group who demonstrated leadership skills to be the pastor.[11] In a brand-new project in Alzenau, Bavaria, the leader was already part of the community; the core team is now getting started and will be led by a Mosaik pastor.

An overview of the current projects is as follows:

| CHURCH | MODEL | DESCRIPTION |
|---|---|---|
| #1 Frankfurt-North (Eschersheim) | Pioneer-Startteam | Pioneer gathers local start team: group decides on Philosophy of Ministry. Every year new trainees brought into the congregation |
| #2 Frankfurt-Northeast | Amalgamation | Existing group is newly planted by becoming multi-site church of #1. Eventually new pastor called as part of greater network. He brings new trainees into the congregation. |
| #3 Oberursel | Amalgamation | Existing group is newly planted by becoming multi-site church of #1. Eventually new pastor/planter called. He, in turn, brings new trainee into the congregation. |
| #4 Gießen | Out of House Church | House church of #1 grows, multiplies, forms central worship service in different city. Leaders |

| | | trained partly in #1 and #3 churches. |
|---|---|---|
| #5 Offenbach | Pioneer-Startteam | Leader trained in #1 church. Forms start-team in part from people of #1 church. Much networking leads to formation of new congregation. |
| #6 Frankfurt-Nordwest | Pioneer-Startteam | Leader trained in #1, then #2 church. Forms start-team in part from people of #1 church. Much networking leads to formation of new congregation. |
| #7 Frankfurt-Zentrum | Pioneer-Startteam | Leader trained in #1 church. Gathers start-team. Much networking. |
| #8 Gießen-South | Collective | Local pastors call on own people to form a start-team under the leadership of one of the local pastors, in order to begin church with a mosaic-DNA. |
| #9 Frankfurt-Heddernheim | Fresh Expressions of Church | Trainee in #1 church invites refugees to gather for brunch, German through-the-Bible and children's program. Organizes team of co- |

| | | |
|---|---|---|
| | | workers out of #1 church. A form of hybrid church runs parallel to #1 church. |
| #10 Alzenau, Bavaria | Core Grooup | Group of Christians from different churches together for 5 years, encouraged by #1 church to develop into a new congregation. Church planter emerges out of start-team, is coached by pastor of #1 church |
| #11 Frankfurt-Bockenheim | Multi-site | #3 church decides to start second congregation under leadership of its pastor. Trainee to become pastor of #3 church, so that lead pastor can start #11 with a new trainee. |
| #12 Frankfurt-Zeilsheim | Amalgamation | Existing church joined the Mosaik network, will be led by the leader of the nearby Frankfurt-Northwest (#6) congregation and begins as a new work. |
| #13 Aschaffenburg | Core Team, Amalgamation | Core team from an existing church in location, with an FTH graduate as leader (not |

| | | |
|---|---|---|
| | | from the original Frankfurt start team), joins the Mosaik network. |
| #14 Darmstadt | Refugee-based | Contact with a refugee center leads to a trans-denominational project with the Mosaik-DNA; revamped worship services, evangelistic small groups; start team begins a new church parallel to the existing works. Pastor and trainees from #1 church meet with refugees for Bible study. Call local Christians into the mix. A lot of networking to create a healthy start-team. |

## Openness for a variety of denominations

The term "multi-denominational" could give the impression that I do not place an emphasis on structures and commitment. On the contrary, denominations have a significant meaning to me and I treasure their histories, which usually emerged from the fathers and mothers of our faith, who sacrificed so much to protect their theological convictions (see Chapter 9). Therefore, from the beginning, we were united in the belief that we did not want to proceed in this network without a commitment to denominations, and also that we did not want to start our own denomination.

The decisive factor for our little movement was that we had learned to think beyond the borders of the various denominations, as Klaus and Debora explained for Mosaik Church #5 (see Chapter 1). Instead, we want to be flexible in working together with a variety of denominations. Each project should decide for itself which denomination it wishes to join. This decision should be made within the first three or four years.

This flexibility helps the church planter, in that he can plant his church in the denomination of his choice, and also the denominations, in that they are "offered" new church planting projects by us, with the understanding that they would be willing to pay a third of the salary of the primary church planter. In this way, we develop relationships between the denominations and at the same time "infect" multiple denominations with our "virus" of the mono-multi-principle (see Chapter 6). Additionally, we are able to reach the people who come to our church plants. Since most people these days are biblically illiterate, we cannot pressure them at the beginning with the expectations and complex doctrinal decisions of many denominations.

Here is an overview of the Mosaik churches and the denominations that they have joined:

| CHURCH | DENOMINATION |
|---|---|
| 1. Frankfurt-North (Eschersheim) | German State Church (EKD): Gnadauer Verband – Chrischona Gemeinschaftswerk |
| 2. Frankfurt-Northeast | Evangelical Free Church |
| 3. Oberursel | Pentecostal Church of Germany |
| 4. Giessen | Evangelical Free Church |
| 5. Offenbach | Anskar Kirche (Free Church) |
| 6. Frankfurt-Nordwest | German State Church (EKD) Gnadauer Verband – Chrischona Gemeinschaftwerk |
| 7. Frankfurt-Zentrum | Undecided |
| 8. Giessen-South | Undecided |
| 9. Frankfurt-Heddernheim | German State Church (EKD) – Fresh Expressions of Church – Chrischona Gemeinschaftswerk |
| 10. Alzenau, Bavaria | German State Church (EKD): Gnadauer Verband – Chrischona Gemeinshatfswerk |
| 11. Frankfurt-Bockenheim | Pentecostal Church of Germany |
| 12. Frankfurt-Zeilsheim | Evangelical Free Church |
| 13. Aschaffenburg | Union of Baptist and Brethren Churches |

| 14. Darmstadt | German State Church (EKD): |
|---|---|

## A Great Start Team

I do not want to claim that churches are best planted or led by students, especially by those whose heads are full of theological terms. But these 24 theology students from the Freie Theologische Hochschule Giessen, with whom we started this work, were something special. The gospel had significantly impacted them and they wanted to come to the side of people in humility, instead of trying to prove their theological knowledge.

The group was made up of 22 Germans, one African and one Mexican – not a particularly multicultural group, but rather mostly Germans, who so deeply wanted to be in contact with people from other cultures that they were able to plant a church that looks different from themselves.

Observers over the years have repeatedly suggested that our movement in the Frankfurt region could have only developed because of this great start-team of Giessen theology students, to which six university students came—definitely a luxury that normally no church planter has when he starts. I fully agree, it was something very special to have so many students who were willing to commit themselves to an unusual church planting project during their studies. They were full of commitment, passion, wisdom and maturity, in spite of their youth. They brought musical leadership, desire for preaching and leading small groups, as well as an excitment for evangelism. And above all, they understood and lived the vision. One of these students wrote to me in the beginning weeks, when hardly anything had yet happened: "Even if you don't get to experience this reformation, we will continue to believe this vision, work at it and pass it on to others until it bears fruit."

However, we should ask the question whether it was really such a luxury that the church was planted by my students.

There are a few factors to consider:

- The students lived 60 kilometers from Frankfurt and the workload in their seminary program was so heavy, that they could hardly take part in Frankfurt life and the building contacts.

- One cannot simply build a church with students, who will soon finish their studies and move away. For one thing, the church bank account will quickly fall into the red zone. Students are easy to motivate, but they also lose their motivation quickly when things are hard. If I had had the choice, from which 24 people I would build my start-team, I would have preferred to only have two or three students as a part of the team.

- "Birds of a feather flock together" – when this idiom is true, then our church plant would have been doomed to failure from the beginning. We were constantly under pressure: we knew that we had only two years to develop out of this group of students a core team of Frankfurt adults. I was often asked how we thought we could manage this task. I myself didn't know how we would do this. We prayed a lot, but I still have no answer as to how we could manage this transformation.

- Students bring a lot of drive and energy, but also a lot of work— not more than other start team members, but for sure not less. Susan and I invested uncountable hours in these young adults. We sat in large groups in our living room and talked at length over various topics and challenges, and then prayed for the work. Every week we had the main leaders over for dinner and worked on our vision, our core values, our goals and strategies. We spent a lot of time together in prayer and also in counseling with individual students.

Were the 24 theology students the key to the success? As much as I am thankful for them and for the unforgettable experience, I would still say, "no." If I had had the choice, I would have built the ideal church planting team this way:

- Adults who are firmly rooted in their community, who know and like many people, and who are so well connected with non-Christians, with whom they have already had spiritual discussions, that they can invite these non-Christians to a test worship service of the new church plant.

- People who have money and who are ready to use it for building God's kingdom; who are committed to prayer, who are more interested in passing their belief and love to the spiritually lost than to building a secure financial plan; and who believe that with God, everything is possible, and he can even use their mistakes.

Whether theology students or not, these 24 young people threw themselves into the work and invested themselves after their graduation in the next generation of students. In this way, everything further developed very naturally – a grass roots movement began.

Perhaps this story can serve as a stimulus for Bible schools and theological seminaries, to take part in a church planting movement in that groups of students work with one of their professors or an outside church planter. In this case, it is wise to set a few ground rules, for example, a set grade point average (to ensure that the student's involvement doesn't hurt their studies) and a daily prayer life.

## A Strong Mentoring System

As we already noted under the first point, from the beginning we had a mentoring system that I developed with a colleague in 2006 and applied to our Frankfurt church plant. I functioned as one of the mentors who led and guided the first church planters; I was joined by some of my colleagues from the FTH, missionaries and other experienced church planters, who stood with the students and led them in their work. With this mentoring and assessment system, the students received not only guidance but also many opportunities to practice preaching, leading evangelistic groups, sharing the gospel, and ministering cross-culturally. At the conclusion of their studies, many of the students were ready either to plant a church or to pastor a church already planted. The key was to trust them and entrust them with pastoral work that is usually left to the "professional".

## Outside Missionaries

Frequently it is not easy to find church planting pioneers who are capable and/or able to start something brand new. A further hurdle is to find mentors for these pioneers, since they're not exactly sitting around at every corner. In addition, coming up with the needed funds to pay the church planters and their mentors is always a challenge. Outside missionaries can be a key to providing the additional resources. Of course, we are always on the lookout for capable mentors on location. But missionaries bring several benefits with them:

- They come to a nation with a deep love for that nation. They have a calling from God to be His blessing to that nation. Often, they love the nation more than the nationals do.
- They are trained to analyze culture. Often, they understand a nation's culture better than the nationals because they bring the outsider-view with them.
- They are trained to operate cross-culturally. In a church that emphasizes nationals ministering to immigrants and refugees, missionaries are especially helpful.
- They bring their financial support with them. They cost the church nothing.

- If they are properly trained or schooled, they can mentor young nationals in ministry. This is especially helpful in a cultural situation in which the national has been taught to think small, but the missionary knows how to think big.
- Some (not all) missionaries make good church planters, once they have learned the language well. Because they are financially supported, they can pioneer a church, then bring one or more nationals into the church to train them "on the job". This leads to multiplication.

Honestly, for a couple of years, I operated with the arrogance that I didn't need any missionaries for my ministry in Germany, even though I myself am a missionary kid and became a missionary.

Karen Smith was the first missionary that I allowed to join us. Her ministry has brought unbelievable fruit. Since then, missionaries have played an important role in the development of the Mosaik churches: Three missionaries became pastors of congregations (numbers 1, 2 and 3); a fourth is an elder in Mosaik church #3 and concentrates on building new projects and ministries. Three other missionaries are in churches 1, 2 and 3 and invest the majority of their time in the refugee ministry, focusing on discipleship and multiplication of refugees into church leaders.

At this point, we have missionaries from the United States, Canada, Holland and India in our team; in 2017 we are expecting our first missionary from Africa to join us. We must learn to be thankful for the refugees who are coming and bringing new life to our churches as well as for the missionaries who make the sacrifices to support us in our ministry.

## Christ and Scripture Centered Preaching

Our experiment, which we at the beginning called "Church for all Nations," was supposed to be more than just an opportunity for the church planting theory learned in the classroom to be put into practice. In this "laboratory", the students could also learn and try out how they could more clearly understand God's mission, implement it in their own situation, and explain to others how one constructs the worship service so that the central theme flows through each element of the service. They could also learn how to develop a liturgy that also allows for spontaneous elements, how to initiate small groups, and how one deals with criticism in the church.

In the center of this is the sermon. In a country in which the historic-critical method has for decades robbed the sermon of its worth, we wanted to give the preaching of the Word its rightful place back. I preached twice a month; the students in the preaching team preached the other weeks. Afterwards, we gave each other feedback; it helped to increase my humility as the students of the preacher took their professor's sermon apart.

In addition, we set a few ground rules in place, which we continue to follow:

- The Bible is God's Word, inspired by the Holy Spirit, trustworthy in everything it proclaims, and as a result the powerful tool through which Jesus personally meets and changes the hearer.
- When we give the preached word its central place in the worship service, people will be drawn into the community, because the sermon regularly and powerfully leads to an encounter with God and his message of grace.
- When we preach the Bible text, we ask:
  - What is the message that this text in its original context had for its hearers?
  - What does this text tell us about God, that allows the hearers to recognize that they are God's creation who bear His image?
  - What does the text make clear in an emotional/psychological way, for example, about the hearers' desires and how God fulfills them?

- o What is the relationship between this text and Jesus – how did Jesus fulfill this scripture text and how does that apply to the life of the hearers?
- And what was most revolutionary for the students: we preach simultaneously to Christians and non-Christians; we don't distinguish between an evangelistic sermon and a sermon to build up believers. There is one gospel for all people. Even believers need to repeatedly hear that they need a Redeemer, need to turn away from their idols and focus fully on God, to find in Jesus' work on the cross their fulfillment, significance and security. So, we preach to Christians and non-Christians the same message; in the end, we preach Christ alone.

I am convinced that the primacy that we gave the preached Word didn't just lead to countless conversions, but also laid the groundwork for future growth. People came, because they realized that they weren't just hearing the words of men, but the words of Christ, even when they weren't (yet) Christians.

## Prayer

Prayer has played a special role in the beginning and in the growth of the Mosaik churches. At the beginning, we often sat as a core team together and spent a lot of time in talking, praying and planning. At some point, I made an agreement with the students who were planning to lead the first projects from the initial Mosaik church to spend at least one hour a day to pray for our church. In the meantime, we have made this a requirement for each church planter from Mosaik.

After the first 19 months of the Church for all Nations, our prayers developed into more than pleas for help, wisdom and faithfulness to God's call. We prayed for contacts with the right individuals who could lead us to people who did not yet know Jesus, and for protection from the wrong people, who were too desirous of accomplishing their own plans through our congregation. As Muslims, prostitutes, demon-possessed, atheists, poor and successful people found their way into our worship services, and unbelievable relationships developed, our prayers became bolder. With expectation, we had dedicated prayer meetings and prayed for more of what God had already started. Sometimes we prayed the whole night long and called for regular days of prayer and fasting.

Sometimes our prayers were more on the defensive side: when our "More than Chocolate" team of four young women went into the red-light district of Frankfurt, in order to offer love, friendship and chocolate bars to the women who worked in prostitution, there were always two to three young men nearby to pray for God's protection for our women.

Offensive prayer played an important role in the whole of our work, for example when we laid hands on each other to pray for God's blessing, healing or comfort for each other. In pastoral care we prayed that people would sense the peace-filled presence of God. And when we spoke to people whose language we didn't understand, we would often lay our hands on their shoulders and begin to pray. We were often surprised at how prayer can break through all language barriers.

I do not believe that God waits until we have reached a certain level of prayer before he blesses us. But everywhere that God is blessing a community with unusual conversions, miracles, and amazing developments, there are people who commit much time to prayer. We recognize that God does more when we pray more and do less, than when we do so much that we can't find the time to pray more.

## Expectant Attitude

One last aspect that I believe is a reason for the growth of the Mosaik church is our attitude. I bumped into this secret when I went from the United States to Canada to plant a church in Toronto. Actually, I didn't know that we had a "secret", until a friend explained it to me.

Toronto had the reputation of being a "graveyard for church planters", and even our believing brothers and sisters didn't believe that we could plant a new church there. Many people asked for analysis and numbers to show that our strategy had already worked somewhere else in Canada before they were ready to join in our adventure. But we didn't want to make our chance of success dependent on numbers and analysis, but rather on God and the power of his Spirit. Nevertheless, we put a lot of effort into studying and understanding the Canadian culture and thought processes. The first interested people came to faith and our church plant actually grew into a stable church.

I will never forget how a pastor friend was asked about us and explained our "success" simply with our attitude. God is not a God of form, but a God of the heart. He seeks people who are ready to fully depend on Him and take new steps. This is exactly the attitude I found with the FTH students who were in our start team in 2011. There are four aspects of this attitude that I want to emphasize:

**Faith:** There are a variety of levels of faith. The disciples in the storm on the Sea of Genezareth were not completely unbelieving, but the miracle of the multiplication of the loaves and fish hadn't brought them further in their faith. God wants to give us faith, that he can do something new or even impossible. The people in Nazareth didn't have this faith, so Jesus didn't perform any miracles there. God withholds his powerful work, when believers are not ready to trust him (which doesn't mean that people who are not healed don't have enough faith).

**Flexibility:** the concrete form of the church ministry should develop out of the local situation. Elements like the Lord's Supper, praise, evangelism, diaconal ministry, etc., are firm elements of Christ's church, which can be adapted to the particular context. We need flexibility and not a firm stand that "we've never done it that way before."

**Appreciation:** what value do we place on people who are completely different from us, especially non-believers? Do we have the humility to be able to learn something from them? Do we have compassion for people who are lost in their efforts or desires, or who have developed bad habits? Do we feel honored when these people find their way to our worship services or small groups? Are we ready to answer their skeptical questions?

This happened recently to Lionel in Offenbach. In the middle of his sermon, one of the guests reacted loudly because Lionel referred to all people as sinners. Lionel did not respond in an irritated manner, but rather thanked the guest for his honesty. He saw it as a compliment that this skeptic was sitting in the worship service and had given Lionel the opportunity to rebut his argument. Lionel's explanation was so convincing that the guest returned a week later. When church members understand that non-believers are showing trust in them when they come to church events despite their fears and discomfort, they will grow in their appreciation.

**Celebration**: When we experience together how God our all-too-human members uses as an incubator for changing lives, we need to celebrate. In Frankfurt-North, we send a "thank-you" email to people who visited us for the first time. After the second visit, they are invited to a "welcome lunch" at the pastor's house. At this lunch, we sit around the table, enjoy my wife's cooking, and talk about how what brought each one the first time, and why they came back. When we hear these personal stories, we have to celebrate!

## God's Timing

I believe that we can rightly claim that the most important success factor was: God chooses His times and ways and prepares His people for what He is planning. We were simply in the right place at the right time. As we decided in 2011 to begin Church for all Nations and the 50/50 model, none of us could have known that shortly thereafter the huge flood of refugees would begin, which would bring hundreds of thousands from other cultures to us. The students simply followed the inner prompting of God and stuck with us during the first 19 months when not too much was happening. As suddenly Iranian and Afghan Muslims, instead of Turks, and traumatized refugees instead of long-term immigrants came, the students were ready for this surprise. Their courage was important, but nothing would have happened as a result if God hadn't been at work and led us there.

Since Germany opened her borders for the refugees from Syria and other countries in the summer of 2015, we have had a flood of experiences in Mosaik Church, which I will tell you about in the next chapters. But first we will take a look at the refugee flood, the largest movement of people since World War II. This current people movement is not just the result of one of the worst tragedies of our time, but also opens a brand-new chance for Him, who can make something good from the worst things. Since millions of people, mostly Muslims, have made their way to Europe, we are seeing God at work among nations who were previously almost unreached.

# 3 REFUGEE'S TRADGEDY, GOD'S TRIUMPH

*"When a stranger resides with you in your land, you shall not do him wrong. The stranger who resides with you shall be to you as the national among you, and you shall love him as yourself; for you were aliens in the land of Egypt; I am the Lord your God."*

**(Leviticus 19:33-34)**

*"Each time that I see the sparrows that fly around in this camp, I remember that 'not a sparrow falls to the ground without my Father's knowledge.' These refugees are like the sparrows."*

**Susan Beck, while serving refugees on the island of Lesvos, Greece, 2016.**

## Into the Black Ashes

The stories are horrible, the tragedy is unimaginable. The Islamist drive for conversion through eradication has devastated the lives of hundreds of thousands of men, women, children and babies. Millions of people in Iran, Iraq, Syria, Afghanistan, Morocco, Eritrea, and Sudan are permanently scarred and deeply traumatized: they have seen their husbands beheaded, their wives and daughters raped repeatedly or hauled away into permanent slavery, their sons' organs cut and spilled out onto the floor, their babies hurled against walls, their fathers lying from the chest up in the street after the bomb blew the rest of the body into a million pieces of flesh and bone. The hatred of jihad has created an unimaginable bloodbath.

There is no need to tell the stories of horror in this book. Mindy Belz, for one, has done that quite adequately in her book, *They Say We Are Infidels*.[14] The award-winning journalist, Michael Richter, has compiled and analyzed the tragedy in his book *Fluchtpunkt Europa*.[15]  His accounts take us to the end of 2014. Since the beginning of 2015, hardly a week has gone by in which we haven't heard of more tragedies, seen more documentaries that tell of the loss of life at sea, read the latest journalistic accounts of virtually un-livable conditions in the camps in Greece, Turkey, Bulgaria and Italy, or read of the refugee homes in Germany that are set on fire by right extremists.

For many of us, these are only reports.  For a young Syrian man who showed me a picture of his hometown, Aleppo, in July 2016, with mere skeletons of buildings that still stood amidst the heaps of rubble, this tragedy is his own personal experience.  He himself was tortured, spat on, and ridiculed—even by Greek police officers, as he made his way to Europe.  On a hot summer day, he cried as he told how his friends and family members were either blown to pieces by a bomb blast or crushed beneath the fallen concrete blocks in Aleppo.

At least half of all refugees who arrive in our towns, our doorsteps, our church communities are deeply traumatized. No country has enough certified, state-approved therapists to handle the long waiting lists of refugees who are living day-in and day-out in a deep psychological black hole.  There are barely enough therapists to handle the long waiting lists of nationals needing psychological and relational therapy. For the refugee, the only hope for healing from the trauma is the church.

No politician knows an answer to this problem, no political party in Europe, whether right-wing or left-wing, has a solution for this human tragedy. No political system can change people who hate others (because they don't share the same religion), exploit (to their own advantage) or debase (in order to feel more powerful), and encourage them to love their neighbors, help them, and respect them.

In the middle of this unsolvable trauma, the gospel shines through. God is mobilizing his children in his church to meet these people, sometimes even before they arrive in our communities. One example is Amir, whom I met in a small church in Athens. I had hardly finished my sermon in a little church in downtown Athens, when this Iranian man approached me enthusiastically. Amir had a translator at his side. He wanted me to know his story. We went into a quiet room and sat down with cups of coffee in hand.

Amir started into a long story about how he had come into this church: He and his strict Muslim wife and their three children had fled Iran. Arriving in Bulgaria, the family had no place to stay and no food to eat. After several days, and praying the ritual Muslim prayers in Arabic, Amir became desperate. Allah was not responding. Amir's children were starving. Even his search for food in public trash cans was to no avail. Something inside him stirred and in panic he called out: "Jesus, I do not know who you are. But if you are, help me!"

An hour later, a man knocked at the door of the abandoned house that Amir had found on the outskirts of a village. There stood a man with bags of food in his hand. The man explained that an hour ago, Jesus had told him to go with food to that address and give that family the food.

This was the first encounter that Amir had had with Jesus. There were more. But the encounter that broke him was after he and three other Iranians—two of them followers of Jesus—had started to make the long journey on foot from Bulgaria to Greece. Amir left his family behind, planning to bring them once he found a suitable living environment in Greece. On the road one day, a stranger walked up to him and handed him a Persian Bible. He opened it haphazardly, and his eyes fell on Isaiah 41:9-10: "You whom I have taken from the ends of the earth, and called from its remotest parts, and said to you, 'you are my servant, I have chosen you and not rejected you. Do not fear, for I am with you; do not anxiously look about you, for I am your God. I will strengthen you, surely, I will help you, surely I will uphold you with my righteous right hand'."

Amir was stunned. It was as if the Christians' holy book was written for him. But that was not all: moments after reading the words of God in Isaiah, Amir's cell phone rang. Someone completely unknown to Amir spoke to him in his Farsi language: "Go to a church (the person gave him the address), they have clothing for you." Amir found the church, and the pastor explained to him the way into a relationship to God.

After Amir gave his life to Jesus and was baptized, he sent word back to his wife and children that he had a new life waiting for them in Athens, that he was now a follower of Jesus, and that he could provide for the family if they moved to Greece's capital. Amir's wife was appalled at her husband's conversion to Jesus. She divorced him and took the three children to Norway. "It has cost me everything to follow Jesus" he said to me that Sunday. "My own life has been threatened several times by those who hate Jesus and want Iranian followers of Jesus dead. But in this church, I have my new family. I also have the confidence that Jesus, who took care of me before my conversion, will take care of me every day since my conversion and until I see him personally in heaven."

As I walked away from my meeting with Amir I thought of how radical his faith was, and how inspirational and motivating this faith can be to European Christians who, for too long, have confused Christian living with comfortable living.

## Rising up from the ashes

"How do we become Christians?"

I could hardly believe my ears. Nobody in the other room had explained the gospel to him. Nobody had argued with this Muslim from Iraq and tried to convince him that his religion was misled and misleading and that Jesus was the right way to a relationship with God. At least not as far as I knew. He just appeared in the living room with his wife and five children and asked through a translator to meet with me in a separate room. That's where he fired the question at me, "How do we become Christians?"

I found out that he didn't "just appear". A week earlier, Christian and Damaris and the start team of #8 Giessen-South had held a welcome festival for the 100 refugees that recently moved into their village. On the menu for the evening: grilled lamb! While kids played football and tag in the parking lot, the smoke rose from the grills as the meat was prepared, and 60 adults from Iraq, Iran, Syria, and Afghanistan filled the hall. The 20 Germans covered the buffet tables with good food and hosted the guests with friendly conversation (or attempts at conversation). Then to the cheer of the people, the delicious lamb was brought in on platters, ready to delight everyone's palate. For the next hour, we sat, ate and chatted with each other. Of course, conversation was limited, but thankfully we found a few who knew some English and could translate into their mother tongue. We Germans strategically situated ourselves between groups of refugees in order to befriend them. Then Christian rose, chose two men who could translate from German—one into Farsi, the other into Arabic—and announced:

"Welcome to a country in which you are free to have your own opinion about God, free to discuss with others about God, free to disagree with others and challenge their view of God. We are starting a new form of church in this town, a church in which Muslims and people from every other religion are welcome...and you are welcome, too. Next Wednesday you are welcome to come to my house at 5:00 p.m. and talk about God. You can come and ask questions, or you can tell us about your view of God, or you can challenge the Christian view of God, or you can just sit back and listen and enjoy the religious freedom you have in our country."

Then he pointed to small cards on a table that had his home address and the time of the gathering on them and encouraged everyone to take one. The Kurdish family from Iraq that I would meet a week later was not at this event. But an elderly German couple was, from a different village, where they had met the Kurdish family. It was this German couple that decided they would invite the seven people from Iraq.

That is how it came to this moment in which the head of the Kurdish family from Iraq blurted out the question to me, "How do we become Christians". The moment felt surreal to me. Never had a stranger approached me out of the blue with such a request. "But you don't even know me. Why are you coming to me with this request?" I asked. Then the man explained that in Iraq two of his friends had converted and become Christians. They encouraged him and his family also to become followers of Jesus. To help him, they gave him three books on the life and teachings of Jesus. He read them all. He discussed them with his wife and his children. They all concluded they should become Christians. They went to a Kurdish church nearby and asked the priest to baptize them. But the priest knew that ISIS was on its way to the town. He told the family that the highest priority in that moment was not to be baptized but to flee. And so, they did.

Through the translator I gently asked questions to ascertain how much the parents really understood. They had never seen a Bible, let alone read in the Bible. But they obviously understood a lot about Jesus from the three books they had read in Iraq.

"But they could kill you if you convert to Jesus and are baptized," I said, wanting to test the family's motive.

"Here in Germany we are free," the husband responded.

"Yes and no," I answered. "There are many Muslims who are angry about their countrymen converting to Jesus, and they are watching you. Last year a man who converted to Christianity was stabbed four times in the refugee home by a Muslim. That was near here. The same could happen to you."

"I would rather be a Christian and die than to be a Muslim and live," the man responded.

I began to cry as I heard the urgency in the man's voice. I simply did not know what to do next, so I said: "Can you come back next Wednesday at 5:00 p.m.? In the mean time I will look for a Bible in your Kurdish dialect. Then we will open to the Gospel of John and read about Jesus. After you see what the Bible says about Jesus, who he is, what he did, and the cost of following him, and I think that you understand in your heart, then our church fellowship (I was thinking of the people who had started to gather as a new church a few months earlier as the start team that Pastor Christian was leading) will organize a special worship service in which I will baptize you into the faith of Jesus."

I drove home that night, but I think the tires were a few meters over the surface of the autobahn. I felt elated and had thoughts like "Has God transferred me into the first century and the book of Acts? This is how Paul and Silas must have felt, when the jailor in Philippi ran up to them and asked, 'What must I do to be saved?' (Acts 16:30). Only the Holy Spirit can produce such moments!" I thought about what Damaris said to her husband, Christian, when I reported to them my conversation with the Kurdish family shortly before I got in my car. She said, "I wish we could give 100% of our time to plant this kind of a church!" But I also thought about the Kurdish man and his wife, how they put themselves and their children through an awful journey and heartbreaking experiences, all because they were driven by the longing to become Christians. They had to find somebody in Europe who could lead them into a relationship with Jesus. We felt incredibly honored by the Lord, that he had led them to us.

# These miracles are happening everywhere

"How do we become Christians?" That is the triumph at the end of the tragedy, the question that crowns the trauma. And it is happening all over! Refugees are putting themselves through the ugliest conditions and experiences in order to get to somebody who will answer their question: "How do we become Christians?" Not every refugee, of course. But many! And it really is happening everywhere. From Hamburg, Berlin, Stuttgart, Vienna, Rotterdam, from large cities as well as from villages, we hear the personal stories of conversions and baptisms.

Like in Athens, Greece, where I was telling a pastor friend of mine about Muslims coming to us, many of them having had dreams in which Jesus appeared to them and asked them to follow him. Philip shot back at me: "Wow! It's happening with you guys in Germany, too?" Then he breathlessly explained:

> The other day I finished up my work in our church building and was locking the front door on my way out, when I noticed 10 Syrians standing on the sidewalk a few meters away from me. In broken English one of them asked me if I was the pastor. When I said "yes", the whole group began to smile. The Syrian man went on to explain to me that they had been searching for several hours for our church building. Someone had given them the address, but what is an Arabic-speaking Syrian going to do with an address in Greek letters? They had just stopped at our building a few minutes earlier, because they saw a cross on the building. A passer-by confirmed that they were at the right address.

"That is amazing" I said to Philip, "a real God-thing!"

Philip went on: "When I asked them what I could do for them, they said:

"Please tell us how we can become Christians!" I could hardly believe my ears. Never in my wildest dreams have I ever thought I would see the day when perfect strangers, and Muslims at that, would walk up to me and just blurt out the question, 'How do I become a Christian'."

"So what did you do?" I asked.

> I immediately unlocked the door and took this family inside. I found out that they are in the refugee center at the old airport, which means they walked several kilometers into the city to find our church. I encouraged them to come back in a few days. In the mean time I would look for an Arabic translator, so I could have a decent conversation with them. A few days later, at the appointed time, they came back. They have been back weekly for my spontaneously created baptism preparation course. They are really sincere. I can tell they have fallen in love with Jesus. He means everything to them. He is everything they have been longing for. In two weeks, we will baptize them into the Christian faith and into our church membership.

It is happening all over: God's triumph after the tragedy! God's triumph over the tragedy!

In Rotterdam, Holland, a Muslim from Iraq heard that a fellow-Kurd had started a church for Kurds. The word on the street was that a number of Muslims had become infidels, turning away from Islam to Jesus, and that this Kurdish church and its pastor were to blame. Even in Europe, it was necessary for this church and her pastor to go into hiding.

The Iraqi went on a search for the address of that pastor. With persistence, he found it. He waited until it was dark, because he did not want to be detected. Inside the high apartment complex and outside the apartment door, he rang the doorbell. The pastor's wife opened the door slightly.

"I must speak with the pastor", the stranger said, "Please let me in!"

The woman shut the door without a word. But the Iraqi was impatient; he knocked repeatedly on the door and called out, "I must speak to the pastor, please."

The pastor heard the panic in the visitors' voice and carefully opened the door and asked, "What is it?"

The Kurd blurted out: "Tell me who Jesus is!"

The pastor opened the door wide and invited the man to come in and sit down, gave him food and drink and opened the Bible in Surani, the man's Kurdish dialect. He then said that Jesus was God, who came from God, who paid for our sins on the cross and who rose three days later, and who gives us his Holy Spirit, so we can have a relationship with God, all our sins forgiven, and eternal life

Suddenly, the man fell to his knees and buried his scream with his hands over his face. He wept loudly. He cried for 10 minutes. Finally, when he gathered himself enough to say something, he looked up at the pastor and sobbingly asked, "Why did I not hear this 10 years ago? I could have told so many people in my country about this? I could have told my whole family, so they could know him, too."

## The Challenge on our Doorstep

It is happening everywhere! Muslims are looking for churches and for Christians who will tell them who Jesus is. They have survived atrocities in their home towns, wild seas; terrible sickness; the stench on overcrowded boats; human traffickers; pirates firing their guns; awful hunger and thirst; border guards; treatment worse than pigs being headed to the slaughter; rape; beatings; imprisonments; insults; cold nights and unbearably hot days; long, dusty roads; endlessly long and smelly bus rides...these traumatized people are arriving at the end of their travels at our doorstep to experience the great triumphant moment in their lives, when they get to ask the question, "Who is Jesus?" and "What must I do to be saved?"

This is the cry of the heart with which hundreds of thousands of people are driven by tragedy from their homes and across the seas and lands, to arrive traumatized in our comfortable lives. It immediately moves the church out of its comfort zone into the discomfort of challenges and questions and disruptions and chaos and risks, even disappointments and mistakes and failures. The alternative is to stay in your comfort zone, to shut yourself and your church community off from this flood of strangers; to try to maintain control of your life and your church, keeping things predictable and structured (and somehow also boring).

Or you can leave your comfort zone and let yourself be taken on the biggest adventure you could ever imagine: being part of a life-giving, joy-producing, soul-healing, peace-making, world-changing movement! Just like millions of refugees are daring the ocean's waves to cross to a place where they can ask how they may become followers of Jesus, I am inviting you to dare the great wave that God has initiated, as he brings these people to your doorstep so that you can bring them to Jesus.

When you choose this second alternative, you will move into a paradigm shift: you will become a fulfillment of Bonhoeffer's call for the church for others. You will jump into a whole new adventure, the mission of God in our time, with completely new challenges and a new way of thinking church and mission.

# 4 A MOVEMENT BEGINS

*"Once someone has experienced a mono-multicultural church, he will never want to go back to a monocultural church. It's like when someone has been watching black and white television for years and then steps into the age of color television."*

**Horst Engelmann (German missiologist, Forum Wiedenest)**

Honestly, I am wary of people who cry "revival"! The American part of my Polish-Jewish-German-Austrian-American-Canadian "multiple personality disorder" has especially become cynical towards my fellow-Americans who come to Europe and cheer "revival" every time an Afghan is converted to Jesus, two Iranians wish to be baptized, or twenty thousand German Christians gather to loud worship music in a football stadium. I hear a growl in my soul that sounds remotely like "Ami, go home!"

But by the summer of 2015 I was wondering: could this tremendous wave of refugees we are experiencing, the unique and rapid multiplication of churches in Frankfurt-Rhein Main, the even more astounding reports of hundreds of Muslims being baptized into the faith of Jesus in churches in Berlin, Hamburg, Cologne, and Stuttgart, from free churches to state churches, be a divine visitation of God upon us?

In October of 2015, I sent out the first email to about ten pastors in Germany whom I knew to be experiencing an unusual time of ministry because refugees were coming into their churches and seeking Jesus. The answer came back from every one of them, that they were surprised by this strange development in their churches and that they felt a need to gather somewhere in Germany, share and analyze our experiences and discuss what resources we could use to disciple Muslims to Jesus, who cannot speak our language.

God's Spirit worked far and beyond anything I could have imagined. I met with Horst Engelmann, a former missionary in Tanzania, now a missiologist in Germany. When I told him of my idea, he immediately agreed to help me get this meeting of pastors organized. With great initiative he contacted a number of missionaries and mission boards in Germany that were involved in ministry to Muslims and organized a "think thank" on available resources we could offer pastors at the upcoming meeting. What then happened, felt to me like a fire out of control. Initially twenty pastors had agreed to come to the meeting, then 40, then 60. We organized our plans for the meeting, based on these numbers, but when shortly before the meeting we had over 100 registrations, we recognized that the plan was out of control. When the day arrived, 150 pastors from over all in Germany had signed up to come by plane, train or automobile for the four hours in Frankfurt.

## February 3, 2016, Matthäuskirche Frankfurt

"I stopped counting," said the co-worker at the registration table, "it must be over 180." The word "awakening" shot through my head, although I didn't want to trust this quiet voice. They came from all possible groups: free churches, state church congregations, and so-called Gemeinschaftswerke (the pietistic and evangelical wing of the German state church). They came from cities, smaller towns and villages from all directions; from mission boards, from movements, from institutions. It was supposed to be a four-hour gathering to converse about resources and strategy, that would enable churches to respond to

God's flood of refugees over the land. Instead, we suddenly felt ourselves at the cusp of something new God was doing and was inviting us to participate in.

Horst Engelmann spoke about our decades-long failure to integrate immigrants into our German churches and communities. "As a result", he proclaimed, "it is now our responsibility to accept this flood of refugees as our mission and to adjust our congregations to this 'new normal'." Then I spoke about God's plan of redemption and the role of the stranger in that plan: Abraham as a stranger, Moses in Egypt, Israel as a stranger, called into a strange land and always mandated to care for the stranger, Ruth, who comes as a stranger into the Messianic line to provide the world with the Christ. Jesus as the stranger, who came into our world to redeem us, who were estranged from God, so that we can belong to His community and His kingdom. And then Pentecost and the New Covenant, through which people from all nations are united into one body and made equal members through their union with Christ.

I concluded with:

> Today we are experiencing how this story of God with the nations is happening right before our eyes. I believe that God is sending these strangers, the immigrants and refugees, so that we as Germans may be and extend the Abrahamic blessing (Genesis 12:3) to them. We are called to open our hearts and serve the strangers, show them grace, give them a glass of water in the name of Jesus and open our homes and churches to them. Could this be the time in which we turn our horrible history into something positive? As one pastor said to me, "I long for the day in which Berlin will no longer be known as a curse but rather as a blessing for the nations." God is giving us today this opportunity to be such a blessing!

But Got isn't sending us these refugees just so that we can bless them as a host nation, but also so that we can be blessed by them. The Christians among us will wake up when they see Muslim refugees turning to Jesus and taking the radical step of being baptized, which in their homelands would put them on a death list. When the "monos" embrace the "multis", the "multis" will bless the "monos." That reflects the beauty of what we call the mono-multicultural church.

Our meeting that day ended with a lengthy time of prayer for this new day for the church. Many pastors displayed deep repentance that they had done so little thus far for the immigrants in our land.

## March 2016: Rotterdam, the Netherlands

In 2012, I met Theo Visser. Susan had heard him at a seminar in 2011 on "multicultural church planting" and had told me: "you must meet him. He is operating out of the same vision you have been operating out of." When we did meet in person in 2012, Theo and I noticed right away that Susan had figured us out correctly. Theo had begun a multicultural church planting movement in the Netherlands a few years earlier. Like me, he felt strongly that the church needs to stay faithful to the timeless message of the biblical gospel while reflecting the development of our societies from monocultural into multicultural. He named his network "International Church Planting". To date, ICP is a total of 30 church plants in the Netherlands, all the product of this man's vision.

We decided to begin an annual conference on multicultural church planting in Europe. After all, in early 2012, I was thinking the same for my country, Germany. In 2014, we held our first conference in Rotterdam. In 2015, an even larger number of churches in Europe were represented at our second conference in Frankfurt.

By the time we held our 2016 conference in Rotterdam, the picture of God's work in Europe had become clearer to us. It was the largest of the three conferences in terms of European countries, churches and participants. The pastors and church workers present were Dutch, Germans, Belgians, English, Scots, Irish, Hungarians, Greeks, Italians, and Spaniards. I brought the opening address on the role of the stranger and of the nations in God's plan of salvation and asked that we all view the current developments in Europe as an outworking of this very plan. In conclusion, I exhorted us to think in terms of "mono-multicultural" instead of "multicultural": "We are not merely calling the nations into our congregations. We are giving the mandate for calling the nations into our congregations, for receiving them, integrating and including them, to the national Christians. We are not multicultural churches, we are mono-multicultural churches".

After three days, several plenary sessions and many seminars, we ended the conference with the Lord's Supper. I was asked to lead it. On the spur of the moment, I decided to bring to those gathered in Rotterdam from various European nations a message from the German pastors who had gathered the month before in the Matthäuskirche in Frankfurt, Germany. I spoke of how the German pastors resolved on February 3, 2016, to take God's movement of mono-multicultural church mission forward. At this point, God's Spirit broke our hearts. I began to weep for the church of Europe. Many in the Rotterdam gathering began to weep. Prayers were lifted up to God for our continent. The Lord of the Nations made it clear to us that the message of a mosaic church that is mono-multicultural must go into every European country and church!

## May 2016: Athens, Greece

My colleague, William, and I landed at the new airport outside of Athens. Philip (of whom I spoke in chapter 3) picked us up. He and other young leaders of the Greek Protestant church had been touched by the message a few months earlier at the Rotterdam conference about mono-multicultural churches, as the same wave of refugees that had swept Germany in 2015 was pouring over Greece in 2016. But the monocultural Greek churches had not yet realized the opportunity God was giving them to "go to all the nations and make disciples" (Matthew 28:19) by contacting and integrating the new strangers at their doorsteps into their churches.

Since the building of the new airport for the 2004 Olympics, the old airport in the city had sat completely abandoned. Now it was covered with people. Refugees. 5000 of them. As we drove past it on our way into the city, the old hangars, landing strips, passenger and ticketing buildings, parking lots...everything was covered with people. They looked lonely, lost, distraught. The conditions in which they slept, stood, sat and ate looked horrid. Way too few showers, too little food, not enough room to breathe. The "refugee crisis" as we knew it in Germany was of much greater crisis proportions in Greece! Philip started telling us many sad details about the refugee crisis. It was, as we entered downtown Athens, that our conversation turned to Philip's encounter with the 10 Syrians outside a church building, that group of Syrians who looked for this church building all day in order to ask who Jesus is.

The next day after our arrival Pastor Philip led us to Victoria Square in the center of Athens. He told us how until recently, the refugees had piled into the little square. They would land on Lesbos, take a ferry boat ride across the Aegean Sea to Athens, then walk to Victoria Square. Here they sat, their bodies so tightly squeezed against one another that it was almost impossible to walk through the mass of people and hand out food and bottles of water. They would come for one, or at the most, two days. Then buses would transport them to other parts of the country, or through other countries on their way to Austria or Germany or Sweden...until the fences went up and the refugees got stuck in Greece and Turkey and in absolutely abysmal conditions.

From Victoria Square we walked to a shelter. A year earlier a Norwegian couple had moved to Athens to serve Jesus there. They organized an NGO and a shelter from which refugees were to be served. As we watched the work of Jesus through the lives of his followers, women and children came into the tiny building. Men had to remain outside. Each woman received a cup of tea, clothing for the family, and the smiling face of one of the workers. Georgia, a bright Greek Christian, married, mother of two young children, leads and develops this shelter. As we spoke with her about the ministry she leads and about the medical services that are offered to refugees in the afternoon, we felt like we were interacting with one of God's heroes.

Philip took us to another center the Norwegian couple had opened. This one was for refugee boys who come to Europe on their own. There are many of them. These boys are destined to live on the streets where they are taken into the slavery of the sex trade. The Christian workers in this shelter pull these young boys off the street. As we toured the building, new beds were being installed and rooms were being gutted and rebuilt for additional bathrooms and classrooms. All over the shelter Middle Eastern boys were working at computers, playing chess, or enthusiastically expending their endless energy over the kicker table. I thought of how in 10 or 15 years there would be men in Greece who would call Jesus their Lord and Savior, because in their youth they had come to experience him through the grace, love and generosity of Greek evangelical Christians and the self-sacrificing vision of a Norwegian couple.

There are way too few shelters in Athens, let alone in the rest of Greece, to cover the refugees' horrible plight. But evangelical Christians in Greece have been a model of mercy and kindness.

What had not yet happened, however, was a conscious initiative of churches to go to the refugees and invite them into the life of their congregations. To that end Philip had organized the conference at which I was to speak. The 50 people who attended were pastors, elders, church planters, Christian workers, and teachers of the Greek Bible College. They came from all over Greece, each one of them by invitation only. The conference organizing team had chosen the topics as well as the participants carefully. In a country in which 0.2% of the population is Protestant, in which the Protestants have been ostracized and nationally scorned by the Greek Orthodox Church, in which evangelism is equated with proselytizing and is illegal, one takes great care in organizing a conference.

The first topic I was asked to cover was "What is church planting?" From that I moved to showing from Scripture, "What is a missional church?" But it was especially in the final block of addresses that God appeared to move in the hearts. "What is a mono-multicultural church?" was the theme. I not only gave some of the biblical background I had given at the addresses in Frankfurt (February 2016) and Rotterdam (March 2016), I gave examples of refugees coming to faith in Jesus through their inclusion into churches. I told them of the Pakistani imam who encountered Jesus "right here on the streets of your city, Athens" before eventually coming to Frankfurt, where he was almost stabbed to death for his faith. I included the story of the elder of #2 Mosaik-Oberursel, Clem and his wife, Sylvia, and their example of mercy and outreach to the Roma people and the young Afghan girl; how God used Clem and Sylvia to prepare the congregation for the sudden "invasion" of 40 Iranian Muslims, as the congregation knew how to immediately move into action due to the compassion Clem and Sylvia had modeled for the members. I spoke about the boldness of the young apostolic leader, Kathi, who walked up to a group of Africans on the sidewalk; of the heart and creativity of the 12 German Christians who invited an entire refugee center to a lamb roast, out of which a discovery evening began, where on the first evening a family from Iraq asked, "how can we become Christians?" I spoke of a special time in history, a time in which there is only one ripe harvest field in Europe—the refugees—and that God sending them to us is part of "the fullness of the Gentiles coming in" (Romans 11:25); and that the host culture (monos) is called upon to initiate outreach to and inclusion of the guest nations (multis). I ended with a question:

"God is on the move to the hearts of people from every language, group and nation. This is his time, his move, his mission. Are you ready to step out in faith and in courage and even with a readiness to be persecuted for the sake of these people whom God has brought to your shores, so that they might come to know the God of Jesus Christ through you? Are you willing to join brothers and sisters and churches in Germany, in France, in Holland, in Italy, who are saying: 'We will start mono-multicultural churches, because we believe that we national Christians are to create spiritual homes for the immigrants and refugees? We, the established churches, will open our hearts and doors to the immigrant and refugee, we will become mono-multicultural ministries, as we participate with God in gathering people to Jesus.' Will you join with the Holy Spirit in this day of renewal?"

I did not know how else to end, so I simply sat down at the end of that question. The moderator stood up in order to close the meeting. The first few words of thanks rolled over his lips, when suddenly a man in the middle of the audience interrupted. In Greek he said: "Wait! We cannot end like this. We have been asked a question. We have been asked if we will join the movement of the Spirit in Europe. We owe that question an answer." People in the audience began to mumble. I could not tell whether they were mumbling in agreement or in disapproval that our lunch was now being postponed even more than my long talk had already postponed it.

The man who had interrupted the moderator was an elder of the first and largest Protestant church in Greece. Its building lies directly below the Parthenon. It was there that the ten Syrians had stood in hopes of asking a pastor who Jesus is. The moderator asked the elder to continue and sat back down.

"Let us give an answer!" the elder pleaded. "Let us join our brothers and sisters in other parts of Europe? Who is for developing our churches into mono-multicultural ministries of nationals to the immigrants and refugees? Raise your hand!" Enough hands went up for the man to walk to the front of the small sanctuary and call all pastors and elders to come forward. They called William and me to stand with them. The elder began to pray:

"Lord, we have heard your call to our churches. We have heard your call to join you in reaching out to refugees and immigrants, to open our hearts and our churches to them, because you want to save them, and you want to renew us. Please (and at this point he began to sob) forgive us for ignoring the stranger you have sent amongst us. Forgive us for not realizing that people of other nations are walking our streets, asking for food and shelter, and wanting to come into our help organizations and our congregations, because you have steered them to us so that they might hear about the salvation you offer in Jesus Christ. Give us faith, give us courage, and please give us renewed churches to accomplish your great commission. Amen."

We were all weeping. To me it felt like the prayers of the German pastors in February 2016 had been transferred by God's Spirit to the Greek pastors and elders.

## Summer 2016: Darmstadt

Things were also moving forward in Germany. Our Mosaik Church network was blossoming in the Rhein-Main area. Exciting contacts were being made: in Aschaffenburg, a small church plant under the leadership of a former student joined our network and in Frankfurt-Zeilsheim, a Free Evangelical Church decided to come under the leadership of our church plant in Frankfurt-Northwest. The Mosaik Church in Oberursel renamed itself New Life Church and decided to bring new life in the Frankfurt-West area by starting a second location with worship services in the old university property.

With great tempo we were nearing our goal from 2011, through which metropolitan Frankfurt from the west (Wiesbaden, Offenbach, Oberursel) to the east (Aschaffenburg) and from the north (Giessen) to the south would be impacted by churches with the Mosaik-DNA. The only puzzle piece missing was Darmstadt in the south. "When we have planted a church in Darmstadt, I can retire," I had sometimes joked.

"We met a young Syrian Christian in Darmstadt yesterday", said my American friend who was visiting us for lunch in 2016. We met him in a park and he told us that he had found his way to Jesus and is telling everybody in his refugee home about Jesus. This guy needs a church and he needs discipling!"

Two days later, that Syrian man from Darmstadt sat in our living room in Frankfurt and an Egyptian Christian whom God provided in a wonderful way was translating. A week later, that Syrian man introduced us to other Syrian young men in the refugee home in Darmstadt. Ten days later, this mass of Syrian testosterone came to our worship service in Frankfurt, received Arabic translation from our new Egyptian colleague, and watched 14 Iranians get baptized into the faith of Jesus. After the worship service they came to our apartment for a spaghetti feast. Ten days later Susan and I drove to Darmstadt with Arabic Bibles. We met the boys for a pleasant, sometimes heated exchange about Jesus' treatment of the Samaritan woman according to John 4.

It turned out that they were meeting on Wednesday with a woman who read the Bible with them. Gisela had taken the Al-Massira course and used these videos to introduce Muslims to Jesus through the Old Testament prophecies. For our first meeting with Gisela, she especially wanted her pastor to be present. I was somewhat reluctant, since many state church pastors are against "mission" and reject the absolute truth claims of Jesus.

A few surprises awaited us that evening: Holger Uhde, pastor of the Melanchthon Church of Darmstadt-Griesheim, was not only warm-hearted and personable; he explained to us that there was nothing he loved more than leading people to faith in Jesus Christ. But what he had not figured out yet is how to integrate these many Muslim refugees into the worship services in order to help them grow in their faith and to inspire the Germans in our church to come to know Jesus personally, too.

"How can we be of service to you?" I asked.

"You can put a Mosaik church into my church! " he answered.

That was one of the most surprising moments in my life. Neither one of us was sure exactly what this would mean, but Pastor Uhde was determined to inject his church ministry with the Mosaik-DNA, so that his people would open themselves to the immigrants, and the worship services would become an incubator for people of all nations, cultures and religions to develop a new life in Christ. Mosaik in a state church — that sounded crazy, but didn't we want from the beginning to be a movement in which we "infected" church plants and established churches with the Mosaik-DNA, instead of developing a new organization?

It became even crazier. The Melanchton core group was growing. Pastors from an area within 15 kilometers of Darmstadt were invited to a meeting to develop a regional strategy for a joint effort. The refugees would be invited into Al-Massira courses; new converts among the refugees would go through discipleship courses, and everyone would be included in mono-multicultural church services and fellowship. But things became crazier yet when I met Raza...

## November 2016, Frankfurt

Raza is a former imam from Pakistan, then a radical Islamic missionary to Athens and a persecutor of Christians. After he had built two mosques in Athens, Jesus appeared to him as an amazing light in a dream and turned his life upside down. He returned to Pakistan, where he told his family that he was now a follower of Jesus. When they almost killed him, he fled to Frankfurt. In the refugee home, he told everyone who would listen about his faith and even in Frankfurt, he was almost murdered as a result.

What impacted me and several of my colleagues more than anything, was when this man announced in November 2016, that God had given him the mission of planting 170 churches in 2017. When I pointedly asked Raza, how one man could plant that many churches in one year in Germany, he showed me a diagram on his cell phone: this new follower of Jesus actually had a strategy in place, how he was going to lead Afghans and Iranians to Christ – though he himself does not know Farsi – and they would immediately start churches that would open their doors to Germans and lead them to the Savior – though Raza himself does not yet know German fluently. It was Mosaik's mono-multicultural approach in reverse!

A few of my colleagues and I sat down with this one-time-Saul-now-Paul and asked him how he would accomplish this fete for Jesus. The Pakistani believer showed us his little multiplication chart: he was already training 6 people, who were each in turn already training 15 people. When I looked closely at the chart, I recognized the locations of these church plants: Giessen, Frankfurt, Mainz, Wiesbaden, Worms. With the last three cities mentioned, this new Pakistani believer was serving up the incredible fact and realization, that every city the students and I had envisioned and prayed about six years earlier, as we dreamed about a metro-wide multiplication movement, was now covered.

The "170-in-17" mission was just crazy and humanly impossible enough that I asked Raza if my colleagues would be permitted to mentor him through this process. He immediately agreed. The big adventure just got bigger.

As a result of the February 2016 meeting in the Matthäus Church, several German pastors and mission leaders joined hands in leadership with the desire to ride the movement of God's Spirit through Germany, all of Europe, to Israel, even to other parts of the world. Our country in particular and Europe in general had been a spiritual wasteland for too long for any of us to know from experience how to handle a special movement of God. But we believed it was our calling to call upon all churches in Europe to join the new wind of God's Spirit. We gave the mission of God the name "MissionMosaik": It was no longer about a congregation in Frankfurt called Mosaik Church, it was about churches everywhere becoming mono-multicultural and looking like a mosaic.

# 5 LOVE FOR THE STRANGER

"When strangers sojourn with you in your land, you shall not do him wrong. You shall treat the stranger who sojourns with you as the native among you, and you shall love him as yourself, for you were strangers in the land of Egypt: I am the LORD your God."

**Leviticus 19:33-34.**

The theme of the stranger is a central theme in the Bible. Over and over, the stranger plays a significant role in God's plan of salvation: Abraham was called to be a stranger in the Promised Land and as a stranger he carried in his loins and in his faith the blessing of God to the nations (Genesis 12:3). His faith became an example for faith in the New Testament, faith that wasn't based on belonging simply to the people of Israel but in a living relationship with God. With his grandson, Joseph, the clan became strangers again, this time in Egypt, where they were first well-tolerated, but later were hated and became slaves. Moses was also a stranger in Egypt, and—as that stranger—led the Old Testament people of God out of slavery and into freedom. Ruth, the grandmother of David, was a stranger from Moab, who through the adverse situation of Elimelech's family, came with her mother-in-law to Israel. She had no idea that God would use her—as a Moabite—to continue the messianic line over King David to Jesus.

The bitter experience of their exile confronted Israel again with this theme: after centuries in their own country, in more or less peaceful times, they were far away from their homeland and experienced anew what it meant to be strangers in a foreign place.

Jesus himself was a stranger. Although the people of Israel had returned to their country, Jesus had to leave this country shortly after his birth, to escape the decree of King Herod to murder the young male children of Israel. Taken down to Egypt, the two-year old Jesus was like the Israelites in Egypt over a thousand years earlier: he was subjected to a foreign culture and a new language. But actually, his coming—as the Nicene Creed puts it—as 'God from God' into the world was the ultimate journey of a stranger into a foreign land. Yes, he came unto his own, but his own did not receive him (John 1:11). It is as a stranger that he goes to the cross and dies for us, who are estranged from God, in order to make us family. His cry, "my God, my God, why have you forsaken me", was the cry of estrangement from the Father. The Son suffered this terrible break with God due to our sins on him, so that we, who were strangers to God, might become his sons and daughters.

As Christians, we are also "strangers on earth" as Hebrews expresses (Heb. 11:13). The first Christians in Jerusalem, like their Lord, had to leave the city in the early days of the church and were scattered in all directions (Acts 8:1). Later, Peter would write in his first letter, "to those who are elect exiles of the Dispersion," meaning in Asia Minor.

## Care for the Strangers

It is this story line that helps us understand why the stranger is always significant to God's people. How can we treat the stranger in our midst with less grace than what we who were strangers to God received from him? God would frequently point to this exodus out of captivity and insignificance as a moment to be remembered and as an event to be emulated: as Israel had been treated with grace, mercy and compassion while a stranger, Israel was to show its understanding of and thankfulness for God's grace by its treatment of the stranger in its own midst (Deuteronomy 10:17-18).

And there were many foreigners who lived in Israel. Our colleague in the gospel, Johannes Reimer, has a very significant section in his book Multikultureller Gemeindebau, in which he outlines for us the Old Testament model for the treatment of foreigners in the nation of Israel. It is impressive to me how the stranger was allowed to cling to his own religion while being given equal rights, equal treatment, and an open invitation to be at Israel's religious festivals in order to hear the truth about the one God who would come into the world as a sacrificial lamb, slain for our sins, without being forced to adopt Israel's faith in the Messiah.

Should we Christians today, as "God's strangers," who are called to show love to our neighbor, be less merciful and helpful in our meetings with strangers? Jesus showed us in one of his last discussions with his people, that he identified himself so deeply with the stranger, that we are actually serving him when we care for the stranger: "I was a stranger and you took me in" (Matt. 25:35).

## Universal Salvation

God did not just come into the world himself in the person of Jesus as a stranger, but he calls the whole world to himself. The Old Testament prophets proclaimed this. For example, Isaiah prophesied that "in the last days.... all nations will stream to it and many people will come" to God's House (Isa. 2:2-3). The term "nations" here is used to refer to the people other than the people of Israel. Starting in Isaiah 42:1,6, Isaiah describes the servant of God who will bring light to the people: "It is too light a thing that you should be my servant to raise up the tribes of Jacob and to bring back the preserved of Israel; I will make you as a light for the nations, that my salvation may reach to the end of the earth"

(Isa. 49:6).

Jesus makes it very clear in Luke's gospel that he is the Messiah for all people from all nations, and Matthew's gospel ends with his words: "Go and make disciples of all nations" (Matt. 28:19). At Pentecost, the Holy Spirit fell on his disciples, allowed them to speak in many languages, which led to God-fearing people from all the world, who were in Jerusalem to celebrate the feast, becoming followers of Jesus. The church of Jesus became international, and it has continued to become more and more international ever since.

This theme of the stranger is woven throughout the missions movements of the last centuries; Jesus stated: "And this gospel of the kingdom will be proclaimed throughout the whole world as a testimony to all nations, and then the end will come" (Matt. 24:14). Then he spoke of the coming of the Son of Man and that his angels will minister to the strangers among us. "And he will send out his angels with a loud trumpet call, and they will gather his elect from the four winds, from one end of heaven to the other" (Matt. 24:31). Paul was the first to systematically apply this vision for mission to the nations. In Romans, he writes that "the fullness of the Gentiles [will] come in" (Rom. 11:25), and in Ephesians, he describes the unity between Jewish believers and Gentile believers, that supersedes the old divisions between the people (Eph. 2:13-14): "But now in Christ Jesus you who once were far off have been brought near by the blood of Christ. For he himself is our peace, who has made us both one and has broken down in his flesh the dividing wall of hostility."

Finally, Revelation gives us a view of what all who belong to Jesus will sing as praise to him in heaven. It is referred to as a 'new song': "You are worthy to take the scroll and to open its seals, because you were slain, and with your blood you purchased men for God from every tribe and language and people and nation" (Rev. 5:9). The nations actually come before the Throne of God.

God's dealings with the world have always been a story with the stranger, and since Jesus' coming it is his deep desire to make his church so international that all people groups can come to him.

## Goodbye to the Principle of Homogeneity

What does this mean for individual churches? Should each church collect itself around one particular nationality? The principle of the "homogenous unit", which missiologist Donald McGavran announced in the 1960s, has been our way of doing church so long, we barely noticed how out of sync the church has become with the development of globalization in our cities and towns. McGavran was a missionary in India from 1937 to 1954. He later became professor of missiology at Fuller Theological Seminary, in California, USA, where he had a great impact on missionary thinking and cultural behaviorism.

McGavran spoke of culture groups as mosaic stones. Each mosaic stone has its own world view and way of life. People who make up a particular mosaic stone will not move into another mosaic stone in order to hear the gospel of Jesus. It is human nature to stay within your own mosaic piece. People will hear the gospel and convert to Jesus, when they do not need to jump over language, class, or racial barriers. McGavran called it the principle of "homogenous unit".

McGavran's intention was to help missionaries understand that by virtue of their moving into a new culture, they were moving into a mosaic stone in which people thought, acted and perceived things differently than the missionaries were used to thinking, acting and perceiving. The only chance the missionaries had to communicate the gospel cross-culturally and effectively was to take on the culture of the group they sought to reach.

For a missionary or church planter or pastor in an intercultural situation to insist on his own cultural form (such as the Christian songs from his country or the form of a worship service or particular perspectives about food and drink) is nothing short of evangelistic imperialism.

In 21st century sociology, the same claims are being made about social milieus: whether one is classed with the hedonistic-materialistic group, the civil-middle, the experientialists or whatever other world-and-life-view groups give a society its various colors, people of one culture group will not move into another culture group to hear the gospel. The "we" feeling of every mosaic stone is too strong for a person to feel "at home" in another mosaic piece. Quite the opposite, he will feel like an outsider, either because he finds the culture of the milieu he has wandered into strange, or the milieu he has wandered into estranges him, or both. We must, therefore, create congregations of a specific milieu that can speak to people of the same milieu. At least, this is what is claimed. And it is what I have taught in class for years. It is McGavran's "homogenous-unit-principle".

At the time McGavran was putting forward the homogenous-unit-principle, he was right in claiming that people are best reached within their own culture and language and national heritage. He made this claim in order to rightfully teach us sensitivity in cross-cultural communication, and he underscored this principle as an era in world history was coming to an end but still evidencing widespread residue.

The explosion of new cultures since the 1950s has ushered in a new era in world history. Our cities have become "urban villages", as people groups cluster in booming metroplexes. "Urbanization"—the move of people into cities—has radically changed the world: today a multitude of cultures live in one neighborhood. More and more, people of many different cultures and sub-cultures shop at the same stores, work in the same businesses, go to the same events. With every generation, intercultural marriage has become more commonplace. The younger generations are accustomed to intercultural schools, cross-cultural friendships, and multi-cultural parties.

For too long, we have been so accustomed to the homogenous unity that we didn't even notice that our cities weren't nearly as homogenous as they were at the time McGavran originally described this principle. As a result, churches and communities have hardly reacted to the globalization and the accompanying change of our cities and have held tight to their monocultural churches.

But something new is happening! The current "invasion" of refugees and immigrants into our congregations is seemingly turning each church into a "heterogenous-collection-unit", into vastly different mosaic pieces that are nonetheless attracted to each other.

This mutual attraction is fascinating even to outsiders. For example, Dieter, a non-Christian, who came for the first time to one of our worship services, said: "I sure didn't expect this from church! All these people here from so many different nations and languages talking to each other like this, that's really good. I don't think I have ever seen this kind of community. I like it. I think we are coming back next Sunday."

Is God exploding the homogenous-unit-principle into heterogeneous-unit-churches? There are some indications that this may be the case. The new phase of the massive immigration opens the door for the unit of a heterogeneous group. People of many different cultures can come together in harmony. McGavran himself called his theory into question at a conference in 1972. I believe that it's time to withdraw from homogeneity and open our churches to the nations. God loves the stranger! He became a stranger for us, so that we might draw the stranger to him.

# 6 BUILDING BLOCKS FOR A MONO-MULTICULTURAL CHURCH

"If the church does not identify with the marginalized, it will itself be marginalized. This is God's poetic justice."

**(Timothy Keller, *Center Church*)**

## The Church for Others is here!

By 2015 reports are coming in from all over: the flow of people from African and Middle Eastern countries into our churches everywhere, in large cities and small towns, in state churches and free churches, in churches with a liturgical style and churches with a freer approach to worship. In 2011 it began as a steady stream. Between 2012 and 2014, its waters rose higher and higher every week, as many of us noticed that the wave was streaming right past our front doors. By 2015, the wave reached tsunami proportions in Germany. Train stations, bus stations, markets, hotels, and school buildings were filled to overflowing with refugees. To us they simply looked like homeless strangers who were invading our status quo. In reality, they are desperately lonely, in search of freedom, refuge and the meaning of life. Many came with a new hunger for God.

Tsunamis carry away everything that stands in their path. This tsunami is no different. As we open our hearts to the new thing God is doing with the nations through the refugees, we will see this flood sweep away the church as we have known it. The time of the monocultural church is over! The church's new normal is a mosaic of many different stones in many different colors. It will not only reflect our globalized society, it will reflect God's idea of church from here on to the Second Coming of Jesus and into the eternal state of heaven.

## What will this mosaic look like? What is the mono-multicultural church?

**The Blue Color of the Mosaic Church**: the base culture (mono)

We have claimed that the new normal for the church of Jesus is not monocultural but mono-multicultural. Let's take that apart: On the one hand, the church has multiple cultures represented in the congregation: many different nationalities, cultures and sub-cultures, all with their specific languages. In the image on the cover, these "metacultures" are represented with such colors as red, maroon, brown, purple, and green. On the other hand, there is the base culture of the congregation. The base culture is the culture that determines the language, atmosphere, major cultural modes and style of the congregation. In our stained-glass window on the book cover, the base culture is represented with the various shades of red-gold.

A base culture can take two forms: One, it is any country's grouping of nationals, whether the Germans in Germany, the Dutch in the Netherlands, the Swedes in Sweden, the French in France, etc. Two, it can be an ethnic-specific congregation that exists in a country from which the ethnic group does not originate. This could be the Koreans in a Korean congregation in Germany, Indonesians in an Indonesian congregation in Holland, or Jamaicans in a Jamaican congregation in

France.

Whether the base culture is nationals or an ethnic-specific group, the base culture does not lose its identity nor the distinctives that make it what it is. But in a mono-multicultural church, there is an intentionality that has not existed in the monocultural or multicultural form of church to date. This intentionality changes the church into a mono-multicultural congregation. What does this look like?

- It is a given that the culture of the people who founded the church—whether nationals or ethnic-specifics (in both cases the "mono")—has a primary place and determining effect on the overall culture of the church. Take German culture as an example: Germans like things orderly, organized and clearly defined. They believe in efficiency, thoroughness and punctuality. Other cultures benefit from that. As they enter German society, the German congregation with its German base culture will help foreigners adjust to these basic attributes of the host country.

- Whoever is the base culture ("mono") of the congregation carries the responsibility of creating bridges from the host culture to all cultures in the church. This means the church's base culture ("mono") will want to instill in all guest cultures ("multi") a respect for the language and culture of the host nation.

- If the base culture of the congregation is an ethnic-specific group (instead of nationals), its responsibility is to transition from the use of its own language to the language of the host nation in its worship services as soon as possible. It may want to function bilingually in its services, but the predominant language should not remain its own ethnic-specific language but the host nation's language. Only in this way will nationals feel that there is a place for them in the congregation.

**The Colorful Stones of the Mosaic Church:** the other cultures (multi)

So far, we understand that the new normal of the church in Europe is not an assimilation of all cultures into a melting pot or a blurring of the mosaic pieces' into the colors of other pieces. We are not trumpeting a call for a multicultural blur. The monoculture of the congregation retains its distinctives. It calls all other cultures to integrate into the church without losing their specific cultural distinctives. Instead, and particularly in the church, cultural distinctives are respected and included in congregational life, side by side.

Every culture reflects equally the sinfulness of man as well as the glory of God. The church's responsibility is to lift high every culture's elements that reveal the truth and creativity, the grace and beauty of God.

*This translates into a very specific church culture:*

The base culture shows respect and gratitude toward the richness of other cultures when it recognizes cultural distinctives as an expression of our beautiful, multi-faceted God of the nations. For example, I grew up in Germany and Austria. After many years in the USA and Canada I had forgotten how drab and colorless Germans and Austrians can dress. Upon returning to Germany at age 50 I was shocked to see that the dominant color of dress—at least it appeared that way to me—was black and brown, with a few Lederhosen thrown into the mix. I just figured that the agricultural mindset had decided that the brown, lifeless fields in winter, when nothing is growing, should be allowed to determine the national color of dress. So, I am always pleased when Diana walks into our worship service with her African dress on. It is so bright, so majestic. It has yellow as its base color, and then many other colors adorning the neck-, wrist- and belly lines. I jokingly call her "the African queen", because the beauty of her dress reminds me of the King of kings in all his glory, splendor and majesty.

On the other hand, foreign cultures can bless the home culture by elevating it to new heights. Most will agree that the Germans, Dutch and English are rather stoic when compared to other cultures' expressions of emotion. Football games are an exception, but even there, it takes some beer to loosen up the fans. Why the low emotional level? Certain cultures have placed a high value on the cognitive level of the human, on the mind, on thinking rationally and thoroughly and scientifically. Then again, they have fairly stiff rules, as far as propriety and politeness of behavior is concerned. Put these people into a worship service and you have a square box, within which emotional and physical display are held in check by the cultural background and make-up of the country. This is where more stoical and contained cultures can show gratitude for the presence of more expressive cultures. I have been deeply moved myself, when in our German worship services, I see Latinos falling on their knees and weeping loudly, deeply touched by God's grace through the lyrics of a song; or by the Africans raising their hands in worship; or the brother from India praying out loud and passionately for God's mercy on displaced Syrians. What moves me most, however, is when I see the Germans feeling a sense of freedom to express to God their adoration of him through their emotions and their physical stance: not because that kind of freedom is my own background—it isn't—but because I see how foreign cultures help a national culture worship God in body, soul and spirit. The point is, that when people of foreign cultures bring their customs into a worship service, nationals can expect to be stretched by the different ways that different cultures act, think and feel things. This is good. It may even change us for the better!

The base culture looks for ways to esteem other nations' cultural elements that reflect the richness of our God. Revelation 21:24-26 envisions that the kings of the earth will bring into the new heaven and new earth the glory and honor of their culture. In a way, this is what the church on earth is called to do. As a preface to heaven, the church is a gathering of people of all nations with the glories of their own cultures. This base culture of a church intentionally promotes the special musical styles, culinary delights, and fashion displays. When we do this, not to ultimately put ourselves on display, but to praise God for being the source of all beauty, sound and taste, we are turning our esteem of cultures into a worshipful esteem of God.

The base culture (mono-) of a congregation seeks to integrate its guest cultures into the national culture, so that immigrants and refugees can begin to serve the society that is becoming their new home. Newly arriving multi-cultural people learn in and through the church to integrate themselves into society, so that they, in turn, can serve other newly arriving multi-cultural people by helping them get established and integrated. Practically, this may mean that the language course a church offers refugees will lead those same refugees to help teach the language two years later to newly arriving refugees. It may mean that immigrants who received help from the church upon their arrival join the diaconal team in the congregation a couple of years later to bring help to newly arriving immigrants. It may mean that, regardless of a person's cultural heritage, he finds ways through the church to contribute to the wellbeing of his host city, be that through participation in children's or youth events in troubled neighborhoods, visiting the elderly in retirement homes, or volunteering in organizations that serve the forgotten, the lonely, or the sick. Certainly, immigrants serve their host society by seeking employment and contributing to society through paying their taxes and to the church by giving their tithe.

As a mono-multicultural congregation focuses on the growth and spiritual maturation of each member, it makes it its aim to bring people from many nations and languages into the leadership of the congregation. This can take the form of a mono-multicultural team of elders, deacons, or pastor-evangelists, or all three. Nobody is to move into leadership out of popularity or the need to fill a certain number of leadership slots every year. And never should we put people into leadership out of the motive of having our token-African or token-Asian or token-English-speaker. The biblical criteria for leadership are always one's leadership competencies (1 Timothy 3:1-13; 5:18; 1 Peter 5:1-5), one's spiritual maturity (1 Timothy 3:6) and godly character (1 Timothy 3:1-14; Titus 1:5-9). The point is, that these criteria for leadership apply across the board to people of all nations and cultures, regardless where these people make their home. A mono-multicultural congregation is going to elect people of all nations to its leadership circles, not only so that the entire congregation with all its different national groups and cultural perspectives is represented in the leadership, but because God chooses to enrich leadership circles through the beauty of diverse perspectives.

## The Boomerang Effect of the Multi-Cultures on the Base Culture

The few years of experience we now have with the Mosaik-DNA have shown us that what goes around comes around. As the national opens his heart, his home and his church community to the internationals and serves them with the gospel of Jesus and with deeds of mercy, the blessings on the internationals come back around to the nationals.

We must remember the status quo we have lived in for so long. Many congregations in Europe have settled into an almost routine way of "doing church". It has become easy to be a Christian on the European continent. All you have to do is give in to the pressures of secularism and certain political rights movements, tweak a few Bible verses on the family and sexuality, and stay silent about what you believe about Jesus, and you will get along well with your surroundings. We have become so settled and privatized in our Christian ways and values, that our ears get dulled to the voice of Jesus, who said and still says: "I know your deeds, that you are neither hot nor cold. I wish you were either one or the other! So, because you are lukewarm—neither hot nor cold—I am about to spit you out of my mouth." (Revelation 3:15,16). The worst of it is that many who think they are Christians, aren't (Matthew 7:21, 10:33).

When Muslims, Hindus, Buddhists and atheists walk into our lukewarm congregations, it is like a wave from out in the ocean rolling slowly and unnoticed our way, and then suddenly crashing with a loud boom-and-swishing sound on the rocks of our churches. They decide to convert to Jesus, get baptized, and in their baptismal vow promise to follow Jesus even if it costs them their lives: There is something very radical in their decision. Many of them have already received death threats over their cell phones from people—often in the refugee homes—who are watching them. Baptism for these new converts is similar to signing their own death warrant. But they are willing to sign it because they know it is a death warrant unto new life.

These converts show European Christians that there is no in-between, lukewarm belief. Being a follower of Jesus disallows the attitude of many "Christians": "I make Jesus the Lord of many things in my life, but what happens to my sexuality, my career, and the way I spend my weekends and my money, that is for me to decide." If Jesus is not Lord of all, he is not Lord at all. The radical conversions followed by a radical commitment to Jesus and his teachings create a wake-up call to the nationals. It reminds me of the second Afghan I baptized: he knew it meant he could be killed for his faith. When he came up from under the water, he was so overjoyed, he dove forward and right back into the water. This kind of joy and commitment is infectious.

The national European realizes by the example of the foreigner that following Jesus is a high and costly calling, that witnessing fearlessly for Jesus in public is the normal way to live your Christian life. We have a lot to gain by the presence of foreigners in our churches. We also have a lot of work to do to transform our churches from the old way into the new normal.

## Unity in Diversity

The new era in which we live has opened the door to the

"heterogeneous-collection-unit", a gathering of people of many different cultures into one harmonious congregation. To achieve unity with manifold diversity, we have to go to the gospel principle behind the homogenous-unit-principle, which is: for effective cross-cultural transmission of the gospel, you have to rid yourself of any and all cultural practices that could hinder the flow of the gospel to another's heart. This principle-behind-the-principle comes from the Bible: "to be all things to all men so that by all means I might save some!" (1 Corinthians 9:22). It is impossible, of course, in a setting with 50 different culture groups—the vast majority of those groups coming from other countries—to let every person feel as if he is back in his home culture. In fact, we must get used to a new dynamic in our gatherings, particularly our worship services: if anybody, either from the mono-culture or the multi-cultures, finds 100% of the worship service exactly to his liking, we can be pretty sure that we have failed to be mono-multiculturally effective. One of my German colleagues in this movement we find ourselves in told a crowd of German Christians in my hearing, that if everybody in a mono-multicultural worship service finds 70% of the worship service meaningful to his heart and helpful to his spiritual condition we have an effective worship service. The 30% that people in a mono-multicultural setting will find strange or contrary to their liking is simply the ongoing tension in which we live and love and minister. We have to teach our mono-multicultural congregations to develop this attitude, as personal consumerism is replaced by a love for the other. We also have to do our homework: we can choose the base culture and one or two other cultures, learn about their perspectives, values and lifestyle as much as possible, and then develop cultural guidelines for our way of being a congregation in a globalized world that has moved into our congregation.

To become a heterogeneous-collection-unit of a church, each member in the congregation has to grow. Two things are absolutely essential if we want to successfully relate to someone from a different cultural background: One, we have to develop cultural humility. That means, in effect, we have to learn to value and esteem the other, to recognize elements in his culture and personality that are rich and enriching to us, to take time for this person, to listen to him and his story, and to be willing to learn from him and his way of doing or seeing things. Second, we have to develop cultural sensitivity. This means we have to show interest in him, know what is really going on in his heart, and show sympathy and a willingness to enter into his joys and pain.

Both aspects—cultural humility and cultural sensitivity—can only be gained if we find ourselves in a community of different cultures. If you are in a congregation in which all people are like you, you are not "forced" to learn cultural humility or cultural sensitivity, in order to get along. In a multicultural atmosphere you are virtually "forced" to grow outside your homogeneous bubble and stretch yourself beyond your comfort-zone. You spiritually mature because you learn humility and sensitivity through your interaction with people who are very different from yourself. This underlines why we are calling for mono-multicultural churches. If you take all the Persians who arrive at your church's doorstep and place them into a congregation of their own (i.e. a monocultural gathering), they also would not and could not learn cultural humility and cultural sensitivity.

Therefore, the best way to create a congregation in which members are constantly maturing spiritually through mere interaction with each other, is to create a mono-multicultural congregation. The church that effectively functions as a "heterogeneous-collection-unit" does so precisely because it clings with all its might to the homogenous-unit-principle. But the homogenous-unit is no longer likeness in cultural expression and values. It is the gospel of Jesus, the power of God's love for every man and woman and child, for every nation, language and culture. "God demonstrates his love toward us in that, while we were yet sinners, Christ died for us" (Romans 5:8). This love grips the soul. It is infectious. It turns people who know they are loved by God though sinners, into people who love others, though they be strangers.

That is the love that Dieter felt, as he leaned against the wall and told me, he had never seen such a gathering of diversity operating with so much harmony. The gospel of Jesus the Christ, who went to the cross for men, women and children of any and every culture, sub-culture and sub-sub-culture, is like a magnet to the soul. It is the message as well as the power that draws the lost heart back to God, where the soul's home is. It is the homogenous unit, and it is so powerful that mono-cultural churches will attract people of all nations and become mono-multicultural congregations.

## But the time is NOW!

As we move forward in this mission, time is working against us. If we hope for a new reformation in Europe, there is little time to think through all eventualities before acting. We must act now. We must in humble faith be willing to take steps, believing that God can even use the mistakes we make. Think of it like this:

- Any stranger who visits your congregation and who is not integrated within six months into the life of and relationships within your church, will drop out. He will either try another congregation or—more likely—will give up on church completely.
- Immigrants to a new land are open to new things, including Christianity, for about 12 months. After that they tend to settle into their new way of life. They then feel less need to open themselves to their new context. This translates into a missionary urgency for the church. Regardless of how many or few refugees have come or are coming to your country, the time to reach out to them is right now.
- The wave of refugees is not one of many ripe harvest fields in Europe in our day. It is the ONLY ripe harvest field right now. If we stand by and do nothing, we are bringing a double-curse on our heads: we will close the door to reaching people with the gospel who could not be reached with the gospel in their own country; and we will close the

door to the possibility that their salvation will bring renewal to our own country and churches.

Only if we make the change from mono-cultural church to mono-multicultural church, and only if we make that change now, we will experience the next reformation in Europe. Let's be ready, with humility and faith to take the next steps. Let's take the chance, even when we haven't thought through each detail to the end. What these next steps could look like will be the focus in the next chapters.

# 7 WHERE TO START

"Never before in history have we encountered such an openness of Iranians, Afghans and Syrian Kurds to the gospel like we are witnessing today. This is unprecedented."

**- anonymous missionary working with Muslims**

"When God blesses you, extend your table instead of building higher walls."

**- unknown**

"Love your neighbor as yourself", the second greatest commandment, is the natural outgrowth of the first commandment, "Love the Lord your God with all your heart, soul, mind, and strength" (Matthew 22:37). There is a good reason for that: It is what Jesus did, and it is the way Jesus functions. He in whom dwells the Godhead, loved the Father with all his heart, soul, mind and strength. Out of this love to the Father, he entered obediently into a covenant with the Father to save what had gone lost. He came into the world and made us his neighbor. We were the person in need of Christ.

When we are translated by God's Spirit into a living relationship to Jesus, we begin to do what Christ did because we are "in Christ". It is our passionate love for Jesus (first commandment) that drives us into the world of those in need, just like love to the Father drove Jesus into our needy world. When Jesus was asked, "Who is my neighbor?" he answered with the story of the Good Samaritan (Lukas 10:25-37). In Christ we become the "good Samaritan", who does not bypass the wounded before us but cares for him, even at our own expense.

Since loving our neighbor is part of being "in Christ", it is essential for us to understand the supernatural nature of this mission of love. Jesus approached the first two men he called to become his disciples with the words: "Follow me and I will make you fishers of men" (Matthew 4:19). Here is the essential point: Fishing for people is not a ladder I climb to maturity and when I reach that level I start getting interested in God's mission. It is not an outline I must learn or a book I must read. When you follow Jesus, HE MAKES YOU into a fisherman. The emphasis in Jeus' words is on his action in each one of us:

He gives you eyes to notice your "neighbor": the people around you, their needs and how lost they are. Ask him to open your eyes.

He gives you his Holy Spirit in situations where you are too weak to handle something in your own strength (Acts 1:8). The Holy Spirit will even do the talking for you, when you do not know what to say (Matthew 10:19). Ask the Holy Spirit to be your companion and helper in situations that are too difficult for you.

He may give you direct orders what to do: Philipp's experience in Acts 9, Peter's experience in Acts 10, and Paul's experience in Acts 18:6 reveal a God who personally directs his servants to specific places and people. Recent history is replete with accounts of God meeting people in dreams or visions or words of Scripture or a strong impulse in their hearts.

He will supply you with everything you need to carry out his will: "Walking in faith" means that you act on possibilities not according to what you see is available but what you believe God can make available. Whether it is knowing the right thing to say, or having the money to do something, or having the people to help you, Jesus has made it clear that he is the giver and provider.

Our responsibilities are (i) to plan according to the desire God has placed into your heart, according to the opportunity that avails itself, and according to the ability God has to do the impossible; (ii) to pray constantly, from moment to moment and in every situation, that God gives you the words to speak, the resources to use, the laborer's to help, the wisdom to respond appropriately; (iii) to open yourself to risks, knowing that only God knows what will happen, why it will happen, and how he will use that which will happen, even if what happens looks like a failure. You do not need to know how steps A to Z look before you take the first step. You must trust God that if you take the first step, he will provide what you need to take the second step. We walk by faith and not by sight.

The point is, it is not the task of the disciple of Jesus to turn himself into a fisher of men. Jesus does that. Your responsibility is to follow Jesus in obedience, trusting him to use you precisely the way he pleases to use you, as you reach out to your new "neighbor".

## Take the Initiative

Many people from Western cultures do not like to be spoken to by strangers. To a great extent this is due to our strong individualism and the privatization of faith that secularism has pushed on us. But people from other cultures are different in that regard. They come from group-oriented cultures, where the "we" carries a more dominant force than the "I", where a collective spirit overpowers the voice of individualism. These people will highly respect you, even thank their "lucky stars" if you smile at them, greet them, introduce yourself to them, shake their hand, and welcome them to your country or your neighborhood. From there it is a very small step into conversation about their family, their history, their needs, and—as Kathi showed us by approaching the group of African Muslims on the open street (Chapter 1)—a discussion of their experience with God.

Ask the Lord to give you the courage to walk into a refugee center and ask how you may meet someone to extend a welcome, or to smile at a stranger in the market place and nod a greeting, or to extend a hand to a woman with head covering and ask her if her family is well.

## Be Where They Are

We need to go to where the refugees are: to the refugee homes, to the waiting lines in front of the social services offices, etc. Like Mandy, a young woman in Berlin, who with her husband has opened their home to refugees, and together have gone to the streets to help the new arrivals in Germany, as they stand in line and wait for their papers to be processed. Her account is an example of how our first responsibility is to go where these people are:

Actually, we should take these people into our arms and welcome them into freedom and peace. These people have lost their homes through bombs and violence and have undertaken a dangerous flight to get to us. Instead, they get sent straight into the meaningless, cold, vexatious war of bureaucracy.

Some private citizen, who wanted to get involved, financed two buses for warming. For months, Sunday through Friday nights, they stand there in front of the regional Office for Health and Community Berlin. One bus is for men, the other for women and families...that is where at least a few people (each bus has 60 seats) could get warm for a little while...Others volunteered to bring food, fruit, water, or they served the people tea. Then there were those who brought warm clothes or blankets. Some even picked up people and took them home, so they could overnight by them and get a shower.

From about 9.30 p.m. on, the first people go stand in a row. There's really no chance to sleep, or someone will take your place in line. During the night, the line gets longer and longer. Then, when the gates are opened between 4:30 and 5:00 a.m., everybody starts to push their way forward. People's bones get broken. Some collapse in the crowd. Every night there are people injured. The ambulatory services know this, so the ambulances arrive every morning at 4:00 a.m. And police cars pull up, too.

Amongst the refugees there are also shy people, people who tend to hold back a bit. They don't have the bite to assert themselves...They just sit there in the line for 3 to 4 weeks, 20 hours a day, in front of the Office for Health and Community Berlin. Every evening they take their place in line again. They have to be there early enough in order to be amongst the first in the morning, if they want the chance to have their turn at getting their papers processed.

I have to cry when I stand there in person and have to watch what goes on there and how so much goes wrong for so many. It is a mystery to me how people can endure this and still be friendly.

## Invite Yourself Over

Many people who come to our land have a rich culture of hospitality. Their group orientation means they enjoy the presence of others in their home. They are not used to making appointments or planning the precise time of the guests' arrival. Much is done spontaneously. They know how to live in the moment.

Therefore, an immigrant will feel honored if you suggest to him that you would like to come and visit with him. Chances are, he will even enthusiastically invite others from his culture group over, so that more people can participate in the joy of getting to know you. When you visit someone, plan on eating. Food is the glue of relationships. Most cultures understand food and drink as an honor to serve, even if they have next to nothing. If you are not prepared to eat and drink, you are insulting them; you are suggesting that you do not appreciate their hospitality.

## Invite Them Over

Hospitality has a divine dynamic when extended "in Jesus' name". Our God is a hospitable God: He has opened his heart to us. He spoke about us entering into his heart through a "door", about coming in and eating rich food and drinking costly wine (Isaiah 55:1-2) that is served free of charge and from a heart of grace. He even turned the picture around and spoke of knocking on our door and entering to have deep communion with us around a banqueting table (Revelation 3:21).

When we open our door to people and invite them into our home "in Jesus' name", we are essentially bringing them into the realm of God's grace. There is a spiritual dynamic that is released when we share our food with them, when we extend to them the fruit of the Spirit (Galatians 5:22-23), when we enter into their life situations and needs. It is, as if we—in Jesus' name—are knocking at their heart doors and saying: "If you open to me (Jesus), I will come in and have a delicious gourmet meal of grace with you."

As God sends the nations to us, God is calling us to learn and practice the spiritual power of hospitality. If you think this is scary you are not alone. Remember the group of people in the Frankfurt suburb of Oberursel that became Mosaik project #3 (Chapter 1)? One of the women in that congregation felt strongly that God wanted her to invite some refugees who had come into that congregation over for a meal. But she had numerous thoughts with which she wrestled against the impulse to invite, such as "they are strangers", "I have three little children and their safety to worry about", "my husband is strong but not strong enough to ward off a machete slicing through his neck".

The more she thought about it the wilder the thoughts got. So she prayed. Finally, she mustered the courage and invited four Syrians over to her modest apartment. The day before the refugees were to come, she asked her friends on Facebook to pray for her. She admitted that she was very nervous. People wrote back on Facebook, encouraging her to go ahead. The day after the lunch with the Syrians, she posted this on Facebook:

> It was such a precious day with our refugee friends at our house. Two of them had had dreams of "a man in a white robe" coming to them and ministering to them in some way. Two have seen Jesus perform a miracle in their lives. All four of them were so thankful to be in a land where they can decide to follow Isa (Jesus) if they so choose. They all said that they felt such love and peace just being in the church every Sunday. They felt safe. Wow. Their stories were very tragic, but their hearts are so precious. Pray for these folks who have left everything and everyone they love to find freedom, safety and a new life.

You can give this kind of hospitality! It does not even mean that you have to make a fantastic meal, clean your home to perfection and drive yourself crazy with preparations. You can be hospitable by letting your home feel and look relaxed. You will honor the person of another culture, by offering to let him or her use your kitchen and cook a meal that promotes his ethnic specialty. Your hospitality can take the shape of going with them to the grocery store, letting them select the necessary ingredients for which you pay, then returning to your place for the feast that they will cook and that you will never forget.

Feel free to pray before you eat. You are the host, and foreign cultures will expect you to uphold your religious tradition. But when you do, make it clear that yours is not a religious tradition but a personal relationship to God: pray a personal rather than a written or ritualistic prayer. And when you thank God for the food, thank God also for your guests. That will register personal love to them.

But don't be surprised if what happened to Damaris and Christian happens to you: Remember the Afghans who came to their house for a Christmas Eve feast (Chapter 1)? Before the group left their home, someone asked the hosts if they could pray Allah's blessing on the family. Damaris swallowed hard and pleaded with the Holy Spirit to give her wisdom for the moment. Then she forced a smile and agreed. She knew it was the Muslims' way of wanting to return a blessing on a family that had blessed them in an unforgettable way. As they all began to pray "Allah akbar....", she and her husband silently thanked the Lord in Jesus' name that he had given them the best Christmas Eve ever, and that their four children would never forget this Christmas, and that their home was protected from evil by the one true God.

If you let yourself in on hospitality, you are sure to let yourself in on an adventure with Jesus.

## Do not hesitate to talk about God

Most immigrants outside of western society have not been raised in a secular environment. They do not think of religion as something that must be privatized. Yet many have been raised in a society in which it is not permissible to think individualistically about religion. What you must believe and how that translates into your cultural behavior has been mandated by the state. For many immigrants, therefore, it is a liberating experience when they suddenly find themselves in an environment in which someone freely speaks to them about God and they may freely ask questions about religion or argue with you from a differing point of view.

Susan and I invited a group of Afghans who had recently started coming to our worship service to visit us in our apartment. Seven men, Susan and I sat in our living room. One of the seven men immediately fell asleep on the soft couch. The rest began their barrage of questions. Some of my answers did not suit them, causing the men to ask further questions, only more heatedly. They still could not understand the Trinity, even after my best but ineffective explanation. God dying on a cross sounded to them like foolishness, and one of the men even said so. For two hours they fired cannonballs at me. It got very intense. One time one of the men yelled so loud, the young man on the couch awoke from his deep sleep. When the evening ended, one of the visitors suddenly said through the translator: "This was the best evening of my life." I was confused. He was the man who had yelled the loudest and argued the most intensely. When I inquired how that was possible, he helped me understand: "I have never had the freedom to ask my questions about God. In my country nobody may ask questions about our religion. We are told what we must believe. Thank you for letting us ask our questions and for giving us the freedom to do that."

I was so touched by that expression, that shortly after Susan and I moved to an apartment in Frankfurt, we invited the group over to our new place for another evening of food and religious exchange. This time, not 7 but 11 men walked in out of a cold winter snow. While Susan scampered into the kitchen to make more food for the additional, unexpected guests, the men gathered in the living room for the pre-meal discussion. It was clear to me that the men had sought out someone in the refugee center who obviously knew the Koran and had all the arguments against Christian teaching. He was like a machine gun, firing one bullet after the other at me, while the Afghan guys just sat, watched and smiled. Sometimes I wished I could be in the kitchen cooking with Susan, instead of being cooked over by the questions and arguments from the group leader.

When the food was ready to be served, the 11 hungry Afghans and one man who had lost his appetite—I am hereby referring to myself—all sat down with Susan at the table. If I thought it would be a peaceful meal, I was horribly mistaken. The questions kept coming. The only change in the heated argumentation was that it now took place with pieces of food flying from several mouths through the air. I could tell the Afghans were having fun. In fact, it started to turn into a crazy party atmosphere, when one after the other got up from the table, jumped onto our couch, and took pictures of us all with their cell phones. "I need to remember this evening!" one after the other would say. "It is so nice to talk freely about the Bible and belief and God." The evening ended with hugs and cheerful good-byes.

Several of the men gave their lives to Jesus in the following weeks. The man whose questions had amounted to a barrage of bullets did not show his face again, at least not for several months. Then, on a hot summer day when our congregation was enjoying our annual picnic in a park in Frankfurt, he suddenly showed up. His little son was along, and so was his wife in head-covering. I wondered if an intense discussion over Christianity would erupt again. But it didn't. Instead, I soon heard someone playing a guitar and children's voices filling the air. I looked around and noticed one of our church members with his guitar, sitting under a tree and leading children in Christian songs. I walked over to see who had gathered. There in the front row sat the Muslim woman and her boy. They were clapping joyfully as they were singing along on a song. Then the man from our congregation began to tell a Bible story. The little boy listened intently. Later, after an hour of joyful eating and conversation, the Muslim man got up from his table and walked over to me. I wondered if it was time for the slaughter! He leaned into me and whispered in my ear: "Thank you! This is very good for my family."

Since then, I haven't seen him again, as his family was moved to another place right after our picnic. But I will never forget his words of gratitude, and what a heated discussion about religion can actually mean to someone who never had the freedom to process his questions about God, particularly in a comfortable situation.

## The Gospel is the Best Thing You Can do for the Stranger

When we talk about God, there is only one central thing for us as

Christians: the gospel. After Jesus said, "You will be my witnesses" (Acts 1:8), the apostles carried out the mandate by proclaiming and telling, by performing acts of compassion, and by doing miracles. The gospel is one whole package that comes to expression through a Spirit-filled life of following Jesus in obedience:

- It expresses itself in words, witnessing to the truth and grace of God through Jesus crucified, risen and coming again.
- It expresses itself in deeds of goodness, mercy and kindness.
- The gospel also speaks through acts of justice, such as restoring righteousness, freeing captives, and stopping the killing of human lives.
- The gospel reveals its power through occasional miracles, through special and supernatural interventions of God into our ordinary lives and into the realm of darkness.

A Christian life brings all these facets of the one great gospel of Christ to expression.

Many of us live in countries whose governments and state churches, whether Protestant, Catholic or Orthodox, have resources and helpers to take care of people's needs. Whether it is being done by the state or by the state church, our task as witnesses of Jesus is to be sure that the whole gospel is getting across to the whole person. Ministering mercy to the foreigner and stranger is part of the mission into which God's people are called. Deuteronomy 10:18-19 states: "God defends the cause of the fatherless and the widow, and loves the alien, giving him food and clothing. And you are to love those who are aliens, for you yourselves were aliens in Egypt." But our biggest priority is to make sure that the person in need receives from us the one thing the state or the theologically liberal church will not give them: a verbal explanation of how God has intervened and seeks those who are lost: through Jesus! This is our primary task.

Sometimes this just happens spontaneously. In Frankfurt-Northwest (Mosaik Church #6), the Syrian kindergarten director invited us to show the 22 children the little church building that we were using at that time for Frankfurt-North's (Church #1) worship services. Actually, we were only supposed to tell them the Christmas story, but on that cold winter day as I opened the little church's large wooden door and the children stepped inside, their first look fell on the crucifix on the altar. "Who is that man on the wood?" asked a little girl. So, the story of the little baby in the manger with the donkeys and shepherds had to wait.

"This is Isa!" I explained. "His name is Jesus, in your Koran he is Isa". I went on to explain that he was God in human form. He had come from God because none of us could get to God or be accepted by God, who is good and perfect, unless all our bad thoughts and intentions and attitudes and actions can be washed away, and we be made clean in front of this God. So, on the cross Isa took all our bad things on himself and let himself be punished by God so none of us have to be punished for the bad things we do. If we receive Isa into our hearts as the king of our hearts, then his blood runs from the cross into our hearts and washes us from all the bad things.

None of the kindergarten workers interjected about my explanation being inappropriate to Muslim children. Instead, one of the boys – obviously having given in to the male gene of daydreaming – asked: "So why is this man on the wood?" Now the group heard the gospel of Jesus a second time. After that we proceeded through the rest of the building, answering questions about donkeys and sheep and how a star stood over something as small as a manger to indicate the Messiah's arrival that people had longed for centuries. Before my wife, Susan, treated everybody to homemade Christmas cookies and hot chocolate, the group of mostly Muslims serenaded us with two Christmas songs that the children had learned in their kindergarten.

That afternoon – the children were back in their kindergarten environment – Susan and I went to the 3-storey building next to the building that had divinely and through prayer "withstood" all efforts to be torn down. One after the other, the parents streamed into the little room the mostly Muslim children had decorated for Christmas.

"Mama, Mama, we saw Isa on the wood today!" The little girl who had asked the question upon entering the old church building earlier that day ran excitedly toward her parents who had just entered. Time stood still for me that moment, as I witnessed a 5-year old Muslim girl's adoration of the cross of Jesus. She was not even converted – not as far as I knew – but already she was a witness to the amazing grace of God. I wondered if a mother's protest might follow in my direction, or a father's hot wrath descend upon the director because the kindergarten had allowed instruction contrary to a family's religion. But nothing followed except silence, as nobody apparently knew what to do with the child's loud and joyful outburst.

Two days later, Susan went to the kindergarten. Friday mornings were her time to read stories to the children. When Susan sat down with the group and opened a book, a little boy suddenly said: "Oma Beck, I'm afraid of the man on the wood!" Before Susan could reply, the 5-year old girl's voice rang through the class: "You don't have to be afraid of the man on the wood! That's Isa. And he is God who came to us, who hung on the wood between God and us, and he took all our bad stuff on himself so that God would punish him for our bad stuff and never have to punish us. You don't need to be afraid of Isa on the wood!"

## Develop meeting points with immigrants

There is a lot we can do to bring immigrants in touch with the gospel before they ever come into a worship service. Take, for example, a group of twenty students from the Wiedenest Bible School in Germany. These courageous young people came up with the idea of scraping some money together to rent and renovate a small place in the middle of town. The village where the school is located has historically had a high influx of immigrants. In 2015, a large number of refugees were placed there. So, the students used the newly renovated place to regularly bake delicious goods, make coffee and tea, and set up a sound system for a group of their own highly skilled musicians. They called it "Jesus Party".

The students advertised with flyers around town for several weeks prior to the first "Jesus Party". But especially the people from the refugee center were invited to come. And come they did! And they still do. Every week 30-50 people, mainly refugees, come to hear "Jesus songs", while Bible school students sit at tables with the free baked goods and tea and coffee and host immigrants for German-talk, life-talk, God-talk or small-talk. "Maybe someday this will develop into a church", the leader of the group said. "We will let the Holy Spirit decide that."

The sky is the limit with how creative we can be to set up meeting points with people who are bored, lonely, needy or just plain hungry for relationships. Remember Dr. Behr, the pediatrician who met with a pastor for prayer every Wednesday morning (Chapter 1) that led to Mosaik-Nordwest being given permission to move into the community center? Dr. Behr wanted to use his waiting room so that the children (at least half of whom are Muslim immigrants) could hear Bible stories while they waited for their turn to see the doctor.

Our Mosaik Frankfurt-North congregation answered the vision of the pediatrician. In fact, I decided to give it six hours of my time a week. An exciting routine developed: "Hello, my name is Dr. Beck. I am Dr. Behr's assistant for personal family care. Dr. Behr likes his little patients to hear stories read to them from the Bible while you are in this room. So that is what I am going to do now: I am going to read to you a story about Jesus. If you have a Koran at home, his name is Isa in your holy book."

As soon as I made the connection between Jesus and Isa all doors opened wide. Except, of course, with those little patients who don't want a story because they are busy writing with pink and blue chalk on the wall instead of the little blackboard. In that case, I would sit down and begin to read anyway. I knew two things: One, even parents will be influenced by readings from the Children's Bible. And two, all you have to do is talk about a stream of blood running from Goliath's head, and the bad boy who is writing on the wall wants to drop everything and look at the picture.

Several parents even order their children to stop writing on the wall and sit down and listen to the Jesus-story respectfully. Numerous parents have ended up in worship services with their children, a result of that first point of contact in Dr. Behr's waiting room.

## Go to a Welcome Event (or create one yourself)

In September 2015, Germany developed the word "Welcoming Culture" (Willkommenskultur). In Austria, this was even chosen as the Word of the Year 2015. Many communities organize a welcome event for the arrival of refugees. If your community does, go! Either the refugees are there, and you will have an opportunity to meet them, or you will learn who the refugees are that will soon be arriving. At these connecting events you can learn what the refugees' needs are, and how you can serve them.

Remember the grill party that Christian and his colleagues put together near Gießen? A similar event happened in the Frankfurt-Northeast church (Mosaik Church #2). At a town hall gathering in Frankfurt, Philemon and Linda from the Northeast congregation met and talked to a newly arrived Syrian couple. The young German couple had been married for three years and had decided they would like to serve Jesus by serving a refugee couple. They prayed for God's guidance, then headed to the welcome meeting. They did not know why, but they felt they needed to approach and talk to the two Syrians. Then they invited them to come to their home the following weekend. Happy to be out of the refugee center, the man and his wife ended up spending Friday night and Saturday with the young German couple.

Linda and Philemon invited the couple to come to a Valentine's party at Patrick and Sonja's place. It was supposed to be a formal dress occasion, with a festive meal, and lots of fun and laughter. The Syrian couple declined. They had lost everything on the journey to Europe. They had no formal wear for the party. Philemon contacted a friend whom he knew to be the same size as the Syrian man. The friend was happy to lend the Syrian man a suit. Linda, for her part, called Sonja. The hostess was delighted about the opportunity to do something good for the Syrian woman: Sonja had three brand new dresses. She pulled them out of her closet, laid them down in front of the Syrian woman and asked, "Which one would you like to have?" The woman was deeply moved by Sonja's generosity.

Two very smartly dressed Syrians came to the Valentine's party. They were not the only immigrants there. Sonja and Patrick had invited two Afghan Muslim women, who had started coming to the Sunday morning worship service a few months earlier. Immigrants and nationals, all 20 people had a great time at the party. During the course of the evening, the Syrian couple found out that many at the party belonged to a small church in the northeast of Frankfurt. They were immediately interested. For years they had wondered what Christians really believe and what a church is like. They asked Sonja and Patrick if they could come on Sunday. But the party hosts were immediately distraught. They were planning to drive to Munich with Philemon and Linda the next day and would not be around on Sunday. "No problem", one of the two Afghan Muslim women said, "we can drive them!"

An unusual scenario developed: the Syrian couple went to the Afghan women's place on Saturday evening and spent the night there. Then on Sunday morning two Afghan Muslims brought two Syrian Muslims to church. The Syrian couple loved it, even if they hardly understood anything. The following Sunday they came again, this time with Sonja and Patrick. This time they understood much of what was said, because Sonja and Patrick were able to translate into English, a language the

Syrians understood. On the third Sunday communion was held. This the Syrians had not witnessed the previous two times. "What does it mean?" they asked. Patrick explained. He told them why Jesus died on the cross, and what the breaking of the bread and the wine in the chalice meant. The Syrian man said: "But we believe in this Jesus now. We want to go up front and be part of this."

As the two stood in front of the server and put the bread into their mouths and drank from the grape juice, they heard him say in English "the body of Jesus was broken for you, the blood of Jesus was shed for you." Tears ran down their cheeks, as they felt a mysterious cleansing wash over them and a deep sense of forgiveness fill their souls.

In the back of the congregation a young man and young woman sat in their chairs weeping, as the result of their visit to the welcome event and their hospitality extended to the Syrian couple was playing out in the front of the sanctuary.

## Start a Language Café

What we are learning since the refugee wave began rolling over us, is that extending language instruction to the new arrivals is meeting the "neighbor" at his point of felt need. Many refugees—not all—come to your country in hopes of staying and making it their new home. They want to get work—in fact, many of them become virtually obsessed with the desire for work. It belongs to their self-respect. It allows them to provide for themselves and their families and, in so doing, to become self-sufficient.

But the shock that immigrants always experience is the bureaucracy of their host country. There is a proper and lengthy process of registration. Though politicians are trying to improve the system, it takes excruciatingly long before an immigrant can get work. For example, he can only get an apartment if he can pay for it. He can only pay for it, if he can get work. He can only get work if he has passed a language test.

He can only pass a language test if he has taken a required amount of language classes. He can only enter language school when the government has finished processing his case. For many refugees, this long and arduous system means sitting around the refugee center for two years, completely bored with nothing to do.

But those 18 to 24 months of "captivity" in a refugee home provide the church with a wonderful opportunity to "love her neighbor" by offering language classes. These can be held in someone's home, in the church building, in a public hall, a hotel, even in a local restaurant. Our experience is that locals can be very accommodating about "their" space being used for German classes. This is also a great way for churches of the same part of the city to work together: people from various congregations form a united teaching team in order to provide the needed number of workers.

Karen Smith, together with our first intern, began a German language course in January 2013. The two explored how a German class was being organized and run by a church in another city. Impressed by the curriculum and the method, the two women received permission to implement the same program in our little church plant in Frankfurt.

To this day, this approach to teaching German to refugees is so successful that virtually every congregation described in Chapter 1 has adopted it.

- Every session is preceded by the team members gathering for prayer before the students arrive.
- When the refugees walk into the building, coffee, tea, cookies and a warm, personal greeting await them.
- They all gather in one room, where the class begins with the usual introduction. The leader begins with: "Hi. I am _____, and I come from _____. I am a follower of Jesus. That means, I love Jesus because he first loved me. I and the others who will teach you German are all loved by Jesus. Jesus loves you, too. He wants

you to feel his love. That is why he asked us to teach you German, so that you will experience how much Jesus loves you."

- Then everybody in the group has to say: "Hi, I am ____, and I come from ____."
- After that, the group is divided up into Beginners, Intermediate and Advanced. Ninety minutes of intense learning follow.  Out of these regular sessions relationships develop. It is essential that workers be prepared to foster the relationships by inviting students to their home, meet them in a café, and invite them to their church's worship service, if they feel their congregation is prepared to provide the refugee with a meaningful experience.
- Offer Bible studies

Many refugees want to read and experience the Bible and learn who Jesus is.  Many Muslims know from their own religion that Jesus was a unique, spiritual person and that the Bible is a holy book (even when they believe that it is false in some areas).  Refugees are known to come off the boat onto Europe's shores asking where they can go to know more about Christianity.

There are numerous resources you can use to fill the curiosity of seekers. For people of non-Christian religions there are also excellent resources. You don't even need to know the language.  The most powerful tool you can use is the Bible itself. In it is "the power of God unto salvation for anyone who will believe, to the Jew first, then to the Gentile" (Romans 1:16). It will cut like a two-edged sword (Hebrews 4:12); it is useful "unto teaching, and unto correction" of wrongly held views (2 Timothy 3:16). Many people have never held a Bible in their hand. For them it is a highlight in their lives, when they can wrap their hands around God's revelation, open it, and leaf through its pages. You will be loved by immigrants for bringing them into your living room and letting them go through Bible verses in their language in the Bible you just gave them, while you follow along in your own Bible.

Immigrants are especially touched by the accounts of Jesus in the four Gospels. They want to know who Jesus is. What also has significant impact on Muslims is to go through the Old Testament with them and show them how Jesus fulfills all the prophecies. The theme of the Fatherhood of God, his deep and passionate love for us, his adoption of us as sons and daughters, and how he in his love runs toward us in Jesus the way the father enthusiastically ran toward his prodigal son, is especially powerful for those who come from the religious mentality of a stern and demanding God, and the hopelessness of ever being able to fulfill his demands.

# 8 MONO-MULTICULTURAL WORSHIP

"They devoted themselves to the apostles' teaching, to the fellowship,
to the breaking of bread and to the prayers...praising God."

**(Acts 2:42, 46)**

"This reminded me a little bit of how the Bible describes the perfected
church in heaven, all these different nations gathered here in such
harmony and joy!"

**- anonymous visitor to a worship service**

Let's experience a church service such as it may unfold in one of our
Mosaik churches through the eyes of a refugee. Hamid was newly
arrived from Iran after a dangerous journey over land and sea.

The sign out front indicated that Hamid had arrived at the correct
location. Still, he was nervous. He had never been to a church service in
his life and had no idea what to expect. What he had, in fact, expected
was that his two Muslim friends would go with him. But one had
become sick and the other bailed on Hamid because he had been awake
until 4:00 a.m. playing cards with other Iranians, and now wanted to
sleep. The easiest thing for Hamid would have been to stay in the

refugee home that morning and simply wait another week to try out a church. Things go better in a group. But he was curious. Since getting off the boat in Greece—actually, ever since he was a teenager—he wanted to know what Christians were like. Here was his opportunity.

Before he could reach for the door handle, the door opened. An older man dressed in jeans and a light blue shirt opened the door and smiled. "Hallo, my name is Günther," the man said and reached his hand out to Hamid. Hamid walked through the door. Music and loud voices were coming from a large hall. Beside the entrance to that hall stood a table, with a man and two women in front of it. The woman closest to him noticed him first, smiled and reached out her hand. "Hello, my name is Melody. Welcome!" she said. The Iranian pointed to himself and said: "Hamid". Melody turned and took a page of name tags, wrote H-a-m-i-d on a tag, pulled it off and handed it to the visitor.

Just then, a young man walked over to Hamid and greeted him in Farsi. He introduced himself to the surprised Iranian as Mohammed and explained that every visitor gets a welcome gift, which now Melody handed Hamid. It was a little book in Farsi entitled "The life you have been looking for", plus a German chocolate bar, plus a card that said "Welcome" and on the back a welcome paragraph in 6 different languages, including Farsi. Mohammed smiled at Hamid and said in Farsi, "I am so glad you are here, my brother! Would you like a head set for translation"? Hamid nodded, as Mohammed handed him a head set. "Turn to channel 3 and hear the entire service in Farsi." Hamid agreed and took the ear phones.

Now he followed Mohammed into the large hall. What Hamid immediately noticed was the many different skin colors. He also noticed a group of Iranians. A kind looking man walked over to the Iranians and greeted each one of them with a hug. It looked to Hamid like the Iranians must have been there before, because they seemed to know the man with the kind face. He, too, had a name tag on his shirt, just like the one that Hamid wore. He was Klaus.

In fact, everybody who was standing in the large room or sitting on chairs had a name tag stuck to his/her shirt or blouse. You really could not tell who was new and who was regular, who was important and who was less important. Everybody had the same kind of name tag, and everybody seemed to be worthy of a cheerful greeting from another. When Klaus was done greeting the group, Mohammed drew his attention to Hamid and said something to the man in German. Without hesitation, Klaus let out an enthusiastic "aaaah", as if he had been waiting for Hamid for weeks and was delighted to finally meet him. Klaus took Hamid into his arms with a big hug. Hamid was surprised. He had been warned that Germans are not the kind to warmheartedly welcome a stranger, certainly not with a big embrace. But this German did not fit that profile. Mohammed explained to Hamid that Klaus was the preacher in this church, a little like an imam in a mosque.

Suddenly the music coming through the speakers got loud. Hamid recognized it only as pop music, the kind he was used to hearing in Iran. People understood the song at a heightened volume to mean that it was time to take their seats. Hamid followed the other Iranians to a row of seats toward the front. Looking around quickly he took in again the different skin colors: a lot of white skinned people, some darker skinned ladies—they might be Latinos, maybe they were Roma, he wasn't sure. There were Asian people, too—he could never tell if they were Japanese, or Korean or Chinese or Thai. Others looked like Indians or Pakistani. Then there were people with black skin, either African, Afro-American or from the Caribbean? Many had ear phones, maybe one third of the hundred or so that were present.

The loud music came to an end and a young man stood up and went to the front of the room. He began to speak, and suddenly Hamid heard Mohammed's voice in the ear phone:

> Hello everybody, my name is Berthold, and I want to welcome you to our church. A church is not a building and it is not a

> place. It is people, people of many different backgrounds and languages. So, whoever you are, whatever your nationality, whatever your religion, whatever your idea of God, and whatever your experience with church—even if it is no experience with church—you are very welcome here!

Hamid was surprised! Why would a church be so open to everybody? But then the young man continued:

> We are a Christian church. That means that many of us sitting here today believe that Jesus is the Son of God, that he is God, and that he is God who came from God in order to make a way for us to God.

Hamid was immediately confused. If Jesus is the Son of God, how can he be God at the same time? And what about the Muslim counter-argument that Allah is no father and has no son? The young man continued:

> We are here to worship Jesus because he is God. If you do not believe that Jesus is God, you are just as welcome here as those who believe he is. I am sure, that as you let the truths you hear about our wonderful Savior Jesus sink into your soul, it will stir your heart to see him in a new way.

The Iranian sitting beside Hamid leaned over and whispered into the newcomer's ear: "Whoever is leading the service says that every week." Hamid was surprised: "Do the imams of this church lead the services?" "No", his neighbor responded, "they call them pastors, but the people who lead the service usually are normal people."

Then the young man in the front showed a red card he had just pulled out of his program. Hamid looked down and noticed that the lady at the greeting table had pressed just such a program into his hand. He did not need to open it. He did not know any German, and he could not fill out the red card the young man was asking guests to fill out and stick into a box, because he could not write German.

Suddenly the band up front started to play. German words appeared on a screen that Hamid could not read. He noticed for the first time the instruments being played: a keyboard, an acoustic guitar a young man about Hamid's age was playing, an electric guitar, a bass guitar, a violin that a young man was playing (he looked Iranian), and a middle-aged man on the clarinet. Suddenly many in the congregation began to clap to the rhythm. Then most of the people started to sing. Not everybody. It looked as if people were free to do as they wished. Two people even went to the back and started dancing. Joy exploded in the room.

Hamid wished he could understand what they were singing, when suddenly Mohammed's voice came through the ear phone: "This song is about God's love. The love of a wife or husband, of a friend or a parent may fail us, but God's love never fails us. The river of his love will never run dry. It always flows toward us. God will never walk out on us. He always walks toward us". To Hamid this was a strange way of talking about God. It seemed intimate, almost too intimate. Even while he thought critically about the song's content, he felt a gnawing in his soul, as if he wished this kind of love and this kind of God to be true.

The second song was also fast and in German. Again, Mohammed's voice came over the ear phones as he explained the meaning of the song. Some people were clapping on this song, too. He liked it and felt like he, too, wanted to clap. But that would show the other Iranians that he might be sympathizing with the Christians and their music, and it could cause them to mock or even threaten him. So he stayed quiet and motionless. On the second verse of the song, the language changed. He could not know that—the letters looked the same—but Mohammed explained: "now we are singing about God's love in Spanish." The third verse was in French, at least, that's what Mohammed said into the ear phone.

A third and slower song followed. Then the man with the acoustic guitar called upon the congregation to pray. Mohammed translated: "We want to pray to Jesus and thank him for the great Savior that he is. Pray out loud, in just a few sentences so others can have a turn. Pray in your own language, we love to hear the different languages in which God is praised."

It became very quiet. Hamid was curious what would happen now. Then a woman started to pray loudly in Spanish. After that a man prayed. Mohammed whispered in the ear phone: "He is praying in German, praising God for being our rock on whom we stand secure."

Suddenly Hamid heard a man pray in Farsi. It was someone in the back. Another Iranian. Hamid turned around and saw in the last row several Iranian couples sitting together with a few children. The one Iranian was praying: "Lord Jesus, you are the king of all kings and the Lord of all lords. You are the fullness of God, you are all that my heart has ever longed for." Hamid had never heard someone pray to Jesus in Farsi. It sounded like blasphemy to him. Three other people prayed out loud— one in German, one in English and one in Hindi.

A sound familiar to Hamid started up through the loudspeakers. It was a song in Farsi, the words appearing in German between the lines on the screen. Hamid read in his language about many different nations, languages and cultures coming around Jesus and worshipping him because his arms are as wide as they were stretched out on the cross. He could tell that the people behind him were trying to sing the Farsi words to the song. In fact, they were butchering Hamid's language, completely mispronouncing words. Sometimes they would start laughing at their inability to keep up mouthing the words. But they were trying to honor his culture by singing a song in his language. It was a gesture of openness that somehow matched the openness of the words in the song: people of all nations, come to Jesus! He is the Lord of all nations!

The song was over, people clapped, and then a woman walked on stage and to a lectern on the right side. She spoke into the microphone: "The Scripture reading today comes from John 5" and with that she began to read from the Bible. Hamid could tell that the mood in the service had changed to one of reflectiveness. She read slowly and with feeling. When she finished, she looked at the congregation and said (Mohammed translated), "this is the Word of the Lord." The people said "thanks be to God for his Word!" The woman said, "It is a lamp unto our feet and a light unto our paths." As the people responded, "we praise you, God, our ears are open to your Word, our hearts receptive to your Spirit", the woman turned and lit a candle on an altar in the center of the stage.

The Iranian next to Hamid leaned over to him. Hamid removed the earphone of his left ear to hear his countryman whisper: "they do this ritual every Sunday. I think they do that to honor their holy book." Then he opened Hamid's program and pointed to the words in print that had just been spoken by the woman and the congregation in response.

A video suddenly started playing. Hamid could not know this, but it was the story the woman had just read from John 5. In the movie a man lying on the ground is approached by a bearded man. The narrator of the film was speaking in Arabic. On a section of wall next to the platform, words were shown in Farsi, Spanish and English. Mohammed said that the reading from the Bible was being shown in a movie version called "The Jesus Film". Hamid read the text in his language, casting quick glances at the film. He noticed that the bearded man who had walked up to the lame man must be Jesus. He had a very kind look on his face. Soon the movie ended.

Now Klaus made his way up to the front, laid his book on a music stand and began to talk. Mohammed spoke into the ear phones: "This is our teacher and he will now bring to us the teaching from the Bible." Klaus started into his sermon by telling the true story about a woman who grew up in India in a Hindu family. The story immediately caught Hamid's attention. The woman experienced the kind of difficult family life that paralleled Hamid's childhood. There seemed to be no love in the home. Hamid found himself emotionally engaged with the story about the woman in India.

Suddenly Klaus switched to another story, this one about a man in Germany, who in his later years of life began to regret that he had not been a good father to his children. Divorced and living on his own, he pretended to be a happy man. After all, he had had a very successful career, and had been able to retire two years ago with a huge bank account, two sleek cars and a boat for great vacations in southern Spain. But deep in himself the man carried a sadness around with him: he had not been able to keep the love of his wife, who a few years ago had married a man that—unlike himself—seemed to lack wealth but paid a lot of attention to her. A certain hopelessness came over the successful German in his older years. He would never be able to regain what he had thrown away.

Again, the preacher left everyone hanging in the story. Klaus made some statement about years passing us by, and how eventually the things we lost or threw away or were taken away become deep holes in our souls that we can never fill again. With that he switched to the story that had been shown in the Jesus video. Klaus retold what happened according to John 5. It was the sad story of a man who was lame and who sat by a pool every day. His was a wretched existence. Like many other people he had believed a ridiculous myth that there was healing power in the water when it moved. The myth included the claim that the person who first entered the water would be healed. It was a brutal myth, in a way, because the man in the story was lame. He had no chance at healing, no matter how much he desired it or tried to drag his body with his muscular arms to the water. No chance, because the other people who believed the same myth and waited for the same moving of the water could all walk! This man was completely hopeless! The preacher pointed to the Bible text to show how Jesus came to the pool, specifically targeting the lame man. He himself gave the wretched man what he was unable to secure for himself: the ability to walk.

Klaus now told the people that God wanted us to learn some important things about life through this encounter of Jesus with the lame man. He said: "First, recognize that even the greatest promises in life cannot give you what you want most". "Secondly, you will never know what you really want most until you meet Jesus". "Thirdly, what you thought you needed most will probably become unimportant to you once you have met Jesus".

Now the preacher moved back to the story of the Hindu woman and her encounter with a Christian woman in university. Then he went back to the German man who had thrown away his family relationships. He explained how both people experienced new life when they met Jesus. The Hindu woman, in fact, became a Christian and started to call Jesus her "guru". Just then Klaus ended with the statement: "You can keep trying to get to the pool in order to get what the pool will not give you; or you can latch on to Jesus, who made his way to you to give you what you cannot get anywhere else. Life will always present you with the decision between the pool and Jesus. There are no alternatives." Then he walked off the stage.

It was quiet in the sanctuary. For a whole minute nobody moved. Nobody said anything. Then the lights suddenly went down, as a reddish light beam shone on a cross that was standing to the back of the stage. The woman who played the keyboard and the man who played the violin appeared on the stage—one could hardly see them in the dark—and they began to play a melancholy tune. Hamid felt himself emotionally drawn in. He thought about the beatings he used to endure in jail in Iran, the deep longing he had felt for freedom. He thought about the awful trip across the ocean. He witnessed a group of Muslims throw people overboard because they were Christians. He thought about the months' long journey on foot and bus through Macedonia, Serbia, Hungary, and Austria, into Germany. He longed to get ahead, to learn the language, to get a good job. But what if he got all those things? Would it be just like that pool that the lame man had thought could heal him, but in the end could not give him what he wanted? Yesterday, when he walked out of the refugee center, a woman across the street had started to shout angry words at him. Had he fled from one hell to another? He felt a lump in his throat, surprised at his own emotional state. Nobody may know that he was afraid, least of all the Iranians sitting beside him. For a moment he felt like he had fallen into a dark hole and was in a continuous fall. Wherever he went the evil in human nature was waiting for him.

The young man who had started the worship service now stood in front of a table with a white table cloth on it. With Mohammed's translation in his ears, Hamid understood the man to be saying that the classical music piece that they had just heard reminded him of life: life without God is like a beautiful piece of music played in a minor key, life with God is that same piece of music played in a major key. What turned life from minor to major and from hopelessness to hope was the crucifixion and resurrection of Jesus. He then invited everyone who was a follower of Jesus to come forward, to tear a piece of bread out of the loaf, to dip it into the cup of wine, and in so doing identify himself with Jesus in the full knowledge that Jesus was identifying himself completely with each person, with all their suffering, with all their longings in life.

Hamid's thoughts drifted away. If God was as merciful as they always said in Islam he is, why does he remain so far removed? Why does this Jesus sound more like what Hamid always wished God would be like? The young Iranian was in deep thought and missed what Mohammed was saying in the ear phones. Suddenly everybody stood up. Hamid quickly did, too, hopeful that nobody had noticed his inattentiveness. That was the kind of religious disrespect his father used to beat him for. But nobody was watching Hamid. He knew that because as he quickly looked around to see if everyone was staring at him, everybody was, instead, taking a sheet of paper out of their program. He quickly reached for his and opened it. There lay a paper with something written on it in different languages. He looked down the page and suddenly saw his language, Farsi. People were now following the young man's lead and were reading the paragraph. Different languages echoed through the room simultaneously. He began to mumble the paragraph written in his language: "I believe in God the Father, Almighty, Maker of heaven and earth, and in Jesus Christ..." He stopped. He didn't believe in Jesus Christ! So he read through the rest quietly. He didn't believe that, either: crucified...forgiveness of sins...Hamid wondered how sins could be forgiven? That sounded so easy, as if there were nothing one needed to do for God to be merciful. Everyone said "Amen" at the same time. Hamid did not know the meaning of that word.

Things went from strange to stranger: the young man took a loaf of bread and a chalice into his hands, raised them up high, closed his eyes and began to pray. Mohammed translated: "God, you sent your Son to be born a child, that we might become children of God. You sent your Son to live, that we might die to ourselves. You sent your Son to die that we might live, and you sent your Son to rise from the dead, that we might have the hope of living forever. We celebrate the feast of God in union with Jesus, the Lamb of God, for whom we give you thanks. Amen." Hamid thought that the prayer had sounded beautiful, even felt beautiful to his soul. But he did not know the meaning of it.

A man and a woman walked forward. The young man leading the service placed both bread and a chalice into their hands. Then people started to get out of their seats and slowly walk forward. The full band began to play, words appeared on the screen, and people began to sing, as one after the other streamed to the front. Mohammed spoke into the ear phones: "The servers are saying to everybody who takes the bread and dips it into the wine or grape juice, 'the body of Jesus broken for you, the blood of Jesus shed for you'." There must be special meaning in those words, Hamid thought, because they kept repeating them. They did something else: they always started that sentence with the person's name, as if the sentence was meant for that person alone. Whatever this ritual was that was being celebrated, it was meant for each individual personally.

Hamid noticed that some of the people going forward were crying. Maybe they had sad lives like his own? Or maybe their tears had something to do with Jesus? He did not know. He leaned over to the Iranian next to him: "Do they do this a lot?" The Muslim whispered:

"not every Sunday but most Sundays. It is a little strange, because we were always taught that this Jesus never died on the cross. But for them, it is the most important thing about their religion." Hamid could not imagine ever getting so emotional about Mohammed or Allah that he would cry.

After the last person had gone forward, the woman who had read the Scripture earlier came to the front and began to pray. Mohammed translated the prayer. When she finished, everybody stood. They took a sheet of paper out of their programs, and read a prayer, which was also in various languages. It started with "Our Father in heaven..." The Iranians next to him were all mumbling along in Farsi..." your kingdom come." When the prayer was over the electric guitar started into a rhythm that had everybody clapping their hands. Everybody began to sing. and Mohammed translated: "Greatest day in history, death is beaten, you have rescued me, sing it out, Jesus is alive! The empty cross, the empty grave, life eternal, you have won the day, shout it out, Jesus is alive, He's alive, he's alive. Oh, happy day! Happy day! You washed my sins away..." This song certainly gave expression to something very deep in these people, something that produced great joy. No sooner had he thought this, they were singing the second verse: "Endless joy, perfect peace, earthly pain finally will cease".

The song ended in a loud, long drum roll. People were actually cheering, like at a sports event. The noise had not yet died down, when the man who started the service stood at the front and lifted his hand and prayed a prayer of blessing on everybody. Then he said: "Thank you for coming and praising God with us. Now let's all enjoy the food and each other's company. We thank the Spanish-speaking house church for putting on a Latino feast for us today." People clapped their hands in thanks.

The Iranian next to Hamid introduced himself; his name was Said. He took Hamid with him to get some food, and before Hamid returned to the refugee home, he was invited to a Persian house group that met every Wednesday.

# Characteristics of the Worship Service

You just experienced a worship service through the sense-experience of an Iranian Muslim who has newly arrived in Europe. I included many of the features of a worship service from Frankfurt #1 church. If you are planning a mono-multicultural worship service, here is a summary of aspects you should be aware of:

## Atmosphere:

One of the most important things a congregation can do is to create a magnetic community atmosphere. Work at the atmosphere from well before the service begins to well after it has ended. The atmosphere must be welcoming – everybody is considered special, everybody is of equal value, everybody is worth inviting over to one's home, an after-service party, or the next event. The way everybody is approached communicates that racial preference, status or caste is a human invention rooted in the evil of self-aggrandizement. The gospel, on the other hand, cuts through separation or preference. The cross of Jesus pulverizes any wall between people and replaces it with intercultural reconciliation.

The atmosphere after the worship service needs to be celebrative: festive music draws people in and creates a good mood; quiet music draws people into deep thought, for example before communion. Songs from other cultures can open our hearts for one another and create a sense of home for people from the "multi" cultures.

The atmosphere after the church service should also include something of a party atmosphere. Good food with good music. Food is God's means of nurturing our bodies, but also nurturing our relationships. Food brings people together, helps them relax and enjoy one another's company. Simultaneously there needs to be quiet corners or rooms where people can go for prayer, counsel, or the moment of conversion to Jesus.

## Culture:

Learn as much as you can about things we might do or say that could hinder the gospel from moving to a stranger's heart: for example, do not lay your Bible on the floor or handle it in any way that could communicate disrespect toward the Holy Scriptures. Muslims view the Bible as a holy book and can take offense at a too casual handling of God's Word. Or clothing: avoid low necklines, holes in your jeans or anything else that could confirm what people in Oriental cultures are mistakenly told about Western women: that they enjoy making themselves sexual prey to men.

## Worship Styles:

No one style is the right one for a mono-multicultural worship service. Our experience over the last years has shown us that immigrants are not drawn by a certain form of worship service, but rather by the love and inclusiveness of the congregation and by the power of the gospel.

The worship service described in this chapter is a blend of free-individual and liturgical-collective. Refugees and immigrants have responded well to the blending of both styles. Therefore, we consciously build fixed elements into our service, such as prayers, readings and confessions that draw all participants into a collective whole, but we also allow for spontaneous elements.

The example also shows that we can introduce songs from other cultures. When you introduce a song from a different culture, it may be best to let native speakers lead the song. Ask your congregation to be patient and not overly critical (for example, when they can't understand the words) and to give space for experimentation. Becoming mono-multicultural in our worship services requires support from leadership and community. Music is an excellent means to draw in people from other cultures—songs in their language give them a starting point and the feeling that they are really welcome.

When we want our worship services to be mono-multicultural, we need the support of the leadership and the whole congregation. An example of this is a particular worship service in which I noticed on the first three songs that the PowerPoint slides were always coming onto the screen too late for us to sing the first line. I found this irritating, and assumed it was irritating other nationals, too. Then I noticed that one of the new Iranians was managing the PowerPoint in the back. When I got up to give the announcements, I said to the congregation: "you may have noticed, that the PowerPoint slides were not always keeping up with the lyrics of the songs. I think we need to celebrate a special occasion today: Payam, who has just begun with German classes, decided to serve this congregation by doing the PowerPoint for us today. Let's applaud Payam for his courage and thank him for helping us in a language he himself is still learning!" This simple explanation replaced any tension with joy. The congregation not only applauded, it cheered for the young man.

## Translation:

In every culture, the translation of the worship service into the languages of the guests is of great importance. It is very challenging to listen to a speaker and to translate simultaneously into another language. Nevertheless, it doesn't have to always be professional translators who do this, since there usually aren't enough of them. Even amateurs can learn to express the essential portions in another language, especially when it is their own mother tongue. In our congregation, we have even used Muslims to translate; some of whom have subsequently come to faith.

For the sermon, it is of great help to the translators when the preacher gives them his manuscript or at least his notes a couple days beforehand, so that they can become familiar with the material in advance. At best, the preacher should also meet with the translators an hour before the service and go through his sermon with them, so that the last questions can be answered, and the translators have the feeling that they are a part of the preaching team. Through prayer together, the preacher and the translators can bless each other for their part in the ministry of the proclamation of the Word.

There are various ways to organize translation into multiple languages. The quickest and cheapest way to offer translation is to organize different language groups in parts of the sanctuary and have a person translate in a loud whisper to the group. If it is just one or two individuals that need translation, they can sit in a row, with the translator between or behind them. If it is a larger group, you may want to move chairs in a circle. The benefit of this approach is that you can do it at no cost. The drawback is the constant drone of talking (translating). Some people will complain about this, saying it is hard for them to concentrate during the service. It is one of many inconveniences a congregation faces once it has decided to be intercultural.

The most advanced and efficient, but also the most expensive way to offer translation, is to build booths with glass windows that you set up in the back of the sanctuary, and behind each sits a translator. He translates into his microphone what he hears from the preacher in his ear phones. Each person needing translation receives his own set of ear phones as he enters and is told the channel number to which he must turn for his particular language. The benefit of this approach is that it reduces the distracting sound of translation. The drawback is the cost of all the equipment. You also must count on technical glitches occurring from time to time. The only way you will ever get rid of all of the background noise that the translation produces is to have your booths completely closed off from the congregation.

## Worship Content:

Did you notice how much was explained in the worship service that Hamid attended? Communion, song texts, Jesus as the Son of God. We can't explain too often what we are doing and what our expressions mean. This doesn't help only the stranger, but also the Christians. "Lamb of God," "sin," "paradise," etc. are all expressions that are not immediately understood today, and Christians also have difficulty in explaining them.

Some things could be explained just by the translator for the foreigners; other things should be explained by the moderator or be printed in the bulletin. Important elements of the service (liturgy, such as the Apostles' Creed and the Lord's Prayer) can be printed and spoken in all appropriate languages, so that everyone can follow along and read them, if desired you can find links to download them in Appendix 3 of this book.

## Preaching:

The results of both postmodernism and globalization have forced us to have to completely rethink our way of preaching. The authority of Scripture and the absoluteness of truth remain unchanged, no matter how much culture and society change. But the way people receive the authority of Scripture and absolute truth today is different than 50 years ago.

Think of it this way: In one and the same audience setting we have a variety of methods of thinking:

- Antithetical thinking (every thesis from the speaker is responded to in the hearer with an antithesis—the logical German way of getting rid of contradictions and ending at a synthesis);
- Linear thinking (the logical way North Americans reason);

- Circular thinking (the more Latino approach of thinking around a truth);
- Deductive-story-thinking (taking principles of truth out of people's experiences—the Indian-Persian way).

You also have Christians and non-Christians in one and the same setting. Among the non-Christians you have European atheists and skeptics, nominal European Christians, cultural Muslims, religiously committed Muslims, Hindus and more.

With this mix of religious cultures, spiritual inclination and mental processing, we need to hold fast to textual preaching (especially since people from non-Christian religions have a high view of the biblical text!), but we may need to invent new communication patterns for each setting.

What is certainly out is preaching mere information you gather from a Bible text, as if you were preaching head to head. You are preaching head-and-heart to head-and-heart and you are preaching cross-culturally, in fact multi-cross-culturally. Many people with absolutely no background in the Christian faith will only decide to accept something as truth if it first moves them at a heart level.

What that means and how we can prepare to address a multicultural congregation through our sermon preparation has several facets:

## Building Blocks of the Sermon

- In your preparation, thoroughly analyze the Bible text, pick the theme of that text and let that theme run like a golden thread through your sermon.
- Begin your sermon with a reading of the text.
- Lift up the theme of the text by telling stories: Bible stories, people's real examples, and personal experiences that move the heart. Let the stories you tell do 3 things: 1. Let them hint at the full-blown action-directive principles with which you will

end the sermon. 2. Let them grab hold of the theme of your Bible text! They provide a certain golden thread that runs out of the passage through the stories to the final principles. 3. Let them highlight doctrinal truths about God. We cannot emphasize "doctrinal" preaching enough: not only European nationals but refugees and immigrants come with very little true knowledge of God. Our story-sermons must be teaching-sermons, through which people learn who God is and how to think God's thoughts after him.

- End your sermon with 2-4 action-directive principles, i.e. tell the congregation what they should do with the golden thread that ran from the text through the stories. Be sure that one of those 2-4 action-directive points clearly shows how Jesus Christ fulfills what the text commands. In other words, show them that Christians and non-Christians alike need Jesus in their lives on a daily basis and for every situation.

- Use visual media! Use PowerPoint in the intercultural setting to strengthen the language bridges. Don't use too much text, but key words, Bible passages, and your action-directive points written out, if possible, in 3-4 languages. With refugees, these are primarily Arabic (Syrians, Iraqis, Moroccans, and Sudanese); Farsi (Iranians and Afghans); English (many Africans and educated people from many countries); French (many Africans); Serbian (Balkans); and Turkish.

# 9 CREATING A MISSIONAL COMMUNITY

"They devoted themselves to the fellowship...All the believers were together and had everything in common. Selling their possessions and goods, they gave to anyone as he had need"

**- Acts 2:42, 44-45**

"Missional" means the local church sees its local surroundings as its primary mission field. It is the natural stance of a congregation: natural, because the church was created for mission; natural, because when the church turns its face toward its surroundings and sees it as its mission field, it is operating like its creator and head, Jesus.

In the past years discussions by church experts and authors have centered around the question whether the missional church is to be "incarnational—the church goes into the world as Jesus' representatives, or "attractional"—the world comes to the church to discover Jesus.

I dare say, if we are to be a missional community, we should not decide between being "incarnational" or "attractional". We are both. The church is the body of Jesus, and therefore it acts like he did: As God incarnate, Jesus went into the world of the lost—that's "incarnational"—then called the lost to himself—that's "attractional".

Incarnational– attractional: The missional community has a go-structure and a come structure. Always! Simultaneously!

What characterizes a missional community?  Here are six aspects that I believe are crucial:

## Welcoming Culture:

In it's "come" structure the missional community is welcoming.  If we go back to our fictional worship service in Chapter 6, we see the following aspects of how Hamid was received:

Hamid felt welcome because of the way he was greeted. As soon as a stranger enters the building where the church is meeting, he should receive a greeting as personalized as, "Hi, I am ____. What is your name?" If the name is "Mohammed Ali Farhad" the greeter will answer, "Wow! Beautiful! How do you spell it?"

A name tag gives the stranger immediate identity. In the first 5 minutes the visitor will probably hear his name 4-6 times as people greet him. The fact that everybody—the visitor and the member who has been coming for 15 years--has the same kind of cheap name tag you slap on a person's chest signals that no matter how long or short you have been in this church community, everybody is the same. Everybody belongs. That is an essential message to the visitor, especially if he is not a Christian nor a church-goer. Everybody belongs, even before he believes.

Another way we can be welcoming is by always being on the lookout for new people. Here we need to remind the regular worship attender to develop a missional habit: have eyes for the visitor! You may want to introduce the 3-minute rule: "The first three minutes after the service, you may not speak to someone you know. Go to someone you don't know". Or if you have a special time in the service for community announcements, ask everyone to stand up and create (what I call) "community chaos" by going to someone they do not know and introducing themselves.

Other ways to be a welcoming community have been referred to in the chapter on worship. You make people of different backgrounds and religions feel welcome when you tell them in the introduction that everybody is welcome, regardless of faith, religion or church experience...when you explain things to them in the worship service they cannot possibly understand, given the background they come from...when you state that everybody is given much space and time to process the truth of Jesus...when you address non-Christians in the service with "some of you are thinking at this point...", and then answer their skeptical question.

It is not always easy to change something in our churches. We have developed structures in our churches for good reasons, and some people react poorly when suddenly something needs to be done in a different way. If we are going to welcome strangers and different cultures into our church community, we need to apply the gospel to something many of us easily turn into an idol: our own local church. What I mean is this: You can handle the church like the man who clutches a piece of gold in his hand tightly and refuses to let go and share it with someone else. When he opens his hand, the gold has turned to dust. When you try to hold on to the church with the attitude: "This is my church, I built this church, these people are my community, these relationships are my friendships, no one has the right to take from me what is mine", you are putting the church into a straightjacket. The result is that it cannot grow, all because you want this beautiful, small creature to stay the same forever. He who wishes his church community to have life and breath and health must release the church from his own clutches and allow the Potter to put the shape to his pottery (our church) as he chooses.

As a congregation we will only then become missional and welcoming to our mission field, when we apply the gospel to our concept of church, open up our tight fists, and share the good of our church with others.

## Integration and Intercultural Reconciliation:

In it's "come" structure the missional community is integrative and supports reconciliation between the cultures. This happens through two levels of community. The slogan we write over both levels is, "large enough to impact, small enough to care."

The macro-level: this is where the church is large enough to impact. The emphasis is on mono-multicultural togetherness and intercultural reconciliation. Gatherings at the macro-level can take several forms.

**The worship service:** When we preach the Word of God, it functions as a judge of all cultures and cultural norms. When we gather to worship Christ the Lord, the worship itself has enough spiritual force so as to reconcile us to one another. Here's how: in the spiritual realm, all people present are gathered up collectively "in Christ". And Jesus has the power to reconcile the world to himself.

When we preach the Word of God, it functions as a judge of all cultures and cultural norms. It calls people of all cultures to repent and turn to him who is the Lord of all cultures. Thus, through the preached Word, there is a congregational turning away from sin and idols and a congregational turning to Christ. People of various backgrounds and cultures are being unified "in Christ" through the common act of repentance.

The Lord's Supper is the experience of communion with the crucified Christ. It is more than a remembrance of Christ, it is a meeting with Christ, a participation of the body with her head, Christ (1 Corinthians 10:16). This has reconciling power.

**Community events:** These are large gatherings of people that contribute to the intercultural reconciliation between people of different nationalities and backgrounds. I remember well the first church picnic that our first three Mosaik congregations had. Amongst many other intercultural happenings, many of the Afghan and Iranian men had gotten themselves together for a volleyball game with a few white guys like me and an English fellow. It was wild, and it got wilder as the sense of competition kept growing. The Afghan and Iranian guys on both sides were having a great time. Amidst laughter, they would high-five each other after causing immediate stomach bloating whenever they stuffed the ball down my throat. The reason I still remember this so fondly is not because the ball tasted good, but because in the world, Afghans and Iranians do not like each other. Iranians think of Afghans as dirt, and Afghans hate them for it. But when they played together on a church volleyball team, they felt a spirit of unity. The most impressive thing that happened was that one of the Afghan players noticed an Iranian standing next to the pitch. He asked the Iranian if he would like to play. The Iranian answered in Farsi, that he would wait rather than upset the equal number of players on both teams. The Afghan walked toward the Iranian, slapped him on the shoulder and said, "Play in my place. We are having so much fun."

The micro-level: At this level the local church focuses on being small enough to care. Here we emphasize community in settings up to 25 people. Like gatherings on the macro-level, the fellowship on the micro-level can take several forms:

- **Task groups:** These are missional communities whose ultimate goal is not the task itself but using a task as a means of bringing people together into a fellowship in which they can come to comprehend and apprehend the grace of Christ.
- **House churches:** I have referred to these several times already. They function essentially as the congregation of the macro-level, only in smaller units. The smallness enables people to disciple one another in the faith, experience the pastoral care they need, discuss and apply the Scriptures to personal challenges, pray and care for each other. House churches can be ethnic-specific, especially when dealing with foreigners who are too new to converse in the national

language or when the ethnic group is one that finds it difficult to integrate (there are cultures that historically have a more difficult time breaking out of their huddle-mentality than other cultures). They can also be fully integrated house churches. Whether ethnic-specific or integrated, the key is to have a person who is a strong pastoral leader, who is continuously trained for the task, and who will lead the group as its lay pastor.

In one of our English-speaking house churches, an Albanian couple with a small child had become very dear to us. The parents had chosen the English-speaking group because they could speak no German. But she could speak some English. On the micro-level, she quietly translated for her husband into Albanian what was being said in the group in English.

When she became pregnant with their second child, she became very sick and had to spend several weeks in the hospital. The American house church leader immediately contacted everyone else in the group. The entire house church rallied around the Albanian family, providing daily meals for the family, babysitting for the daughter, transportation and translation when the mother visited a doctor, as well as emails and cards to express their care. What impressed me was how the American man cared for his own little flock, informing the house church day-in-day-out what the members of the house church could do practically to care for this dear family. What impressed me just as much, was that the lead pastor (at the macro-level) never once was asked to step in and do something. He was kept informed, but like Ephesians 4:12 mandates, the members of the body carried out ministry to the body themselves.

- **Two-somes or three-somes:** If meeting every week is simply too much for people with a busy lifestyle this can be the best approach for constant accountability and spiritual growth. Meetings can happen when the 2 or 3 people who are functioning as a kind of mini-house church have just a few minutes before they have to get back to work. They discuss how the Bible text they had agreed to read impacted them personally, what personal challenges or temptations they are wrestling with, and pray for each other and for their non-Christian friends.

- **Hybrid groups/Fresh Expressions of Church:** These are small groups for people who are not ready for a house church or a larger worship setting. They are open to read the Bible and discuss its content, but their lack of language skills limits their ability to comprehend the content quickly. They can also be people who live in fear that if certain others were to find out they were associating with a church, they would face serious consequences. These people need the kind of group that is described in Chapter 1 as a Fresh Expressions of Church group.

- **Social Media Groups:** Several Iranians in one of our congregations adopted this idea completely on their own. They feel like a group, they come to worship services regularly on the macro-level, but during the week they are busy taking language classes, looking for work, or bringing the gospel to other Persian-speakers. They send What'sApp messages to each other twice a day with Bible verses and encouraging words.

## Initiative

In it's "come" structure the base culture doesn't just wait for people from outside to come and become active. This means that in the intercultural church community the nationals (base culture) take the initiative to move toward the foreigner (outside culture). A certain dynamic leads us to this conclusion: When people of outside cultures enter the realm of the base culture, they feel like strangers because they are strangers. They feel—at least at first—unsure, nervous or afraid. They do not know the culture of the land, and they certainly do not know the culture of the church, any more than a Christian would know the culture of the mosque or a temple when entering for the first time. Consequently, people of outside cultures will keep themselves on the perimeter of the host community.

On the other hand, people of the base culture feel threatened to some extent when the people of outside cultures come on to their turf. We live in a sin-riddled and broken world, and we react to those who are different from us out of our sin-riddled and broken hearts. The natural reaction when two different cultures come upon each other is not to experience a centrifugal but a centripetal force, not to be drawn to each other but to push away from each other. Like the "Ami, go home!" reaction in the post-war years of Germany, it's no different in the post-modern world today: People of the base culture will feel threatened by the stranger because he dresses differently, may smell differently, believes in a completely different god, thinks differently, values different things. At the root of this reaction to the stranger lies fear. The host fears that the community he has built and in which he feels comfortable will be taken from him. He fears that the stranger could cause strange things to develop and accustomed things to be forgotten.

This is where the gospel kicks in: The person of the host culture who is filled with the love of Jesus and the power of the Spirit initiates. He takes the responsibility upon himself and approaches the stranger with a smile and a handshake. He does not wait for the stranger to come toward him with a smile and a handshake. The national approaches the international and invites him into his home, into the group, into his row of seats in the worship service, into the fellowship time after the service. When meeting with German church leaders in December 2015, in a think-tank meeting regarding the church's new mission in Europe, one participant said: "We Germans like to pull back and have our time and place of quiet (Ruhe). We need Germans to be driven by sympathy out of their quiet zone into the world of the stranger."

One more thing about initiating: A year or so after welcoming the first Afghans into our community with great enthusiasm, we began to hear the first complaints from them: they noticed that we were joyfully embracing the newest newcomers, but we were not greeting them each week with as great a cheer and as strong a hug as we had upon their first arrival. They felt that they had become just routine-people to us. As we analyzed their complaint we concluded two factors: we needed to be careful to celebrate everybody's presence in the community with equal enthusiasm, regardless if they were new or a longtime member. But secondly, we needed to be sure to disciple new converts that maturing in Christ means taking responsibility toward the entire community. To put it another way, the problem lay in the above sentence "They felt that they had become just routine-people to us". When we disciple people to be followers of Christ we disciple them to become participants in the missional community. They are no longer the stranger who now has become "just routine-people to us". They have become "us". They are "us". In the name of Jesus, they, like the rest of us, now move toward the newcomer and welcome him into the community.

## Sacrificial Attitude

In its "come" and in its "go" structure, the missional community acts like its King: self-sacrificing, especially toward those who are deemed lesser or are poor and needy. This is based on the nature of Jesus himself. The head of the body said: "The Son of Man did not come to be served but to serve, and to give his life a ransom for many" (Mark 10:45). The body is the extension of its head. It does what the head wants it to do. Jesus wants to serve by giving his life for many. We, therefore, give our lives in sacrifice for the many. Here we see again the inseparable connection between loving the Lord your God and loving your neighbor as yourself. When you love Jesus, you begin to do what Jesus did the way Jesus did it and wants it done.

This self-sacrificial nature is expressed in the New Testament word for fellowship: koinonia. The Greek word describes far more than simply a group of people sitting or eating together. It means a group of people who—beyond sitting and eating together—are also willing to give the shirts off their backs for the comfort of others, and willing to open their homes for the safety of others. The koinonia of the Jerusalem church community is described in the words: "They devoted themselves to...the fellowship (koinonia)...All the believers were together and had everything in common. Selling their possessions and goods, they gave to anyone as he had need" (Acts 2:42, 44-45).

Koinonia is self-sacrificial fellowship. It is looking out for the needs of the other. This kind of community transforms a congregation. And when the dynamic of loving fellowship moves like a sweet aroma into a congregation, God entrusts to that fellowship strangers and foreigners whom he wishes to save.

Nowhere have I seen this better exemplified than in church plant #3 (See Chapters 1 and 2), the little group in the Frankfurt suburb of Oberursel, that amalgamated with church plant #1 in 2012. Clem, whose love for keeping things the same and at even keel is underscored by the "triple whammy" that he is an Englishman who works as an engineer in Germany, and his "let's-just-take-the-bull-by-the-horns-and-get-this-done" fiery Italian wife, Sylvia, had started this fellowship of believers 25 years before re-birthing itself with the Mosaik-DNA. Today people are drawn into this congregation because of the koinonia way with which the members include strangers in their fellowship. What you need to understand, however, is that this church community did not simply develop into a congregation that is loving and embracing toward outsiders by itself. The catalyst for this was none other than Clem and Sylvia Fisher.


Two and a half months after joining with Church for all Nations, on a Sunday morning in January, Clem and Sylvia were getting ready to go to their worship service when their doorbell rang. They found three strangers in front of their door, a middle-aged woman and two young men, who handed them a slip of paper which had Clem and Sylvia' s address on it. After offering them breakfast they took them along to the Mosaik Sunday Service even though they must have understood very little, as they didn't speak any German. Thanks to a woman in the church who spoke Czech it became clear that the three came from the border between Slovakia and Hungary and lived by begging and occasional jobs. Their current home was a little tent in the woods outside of Oberursel. The temperatures outside were well below the freezing point!

After the worship service, Clem and Sylvia packed the three strangers in their car. They drove to the woods. The three homeless then guided them on foot to their snow-covered tents in the woods. Clem and Sylvia "had enough Bible in them" that they knew they could not merely leave the three strangers with their tent out in the cold. They asked them to pack up their few belongings and to stay the night at their home. The next day Sylvia went to the authorities to begin a legalization process for the three and to find them shelter. But all search for a roof over their heads came to nothing. One night's stay developed into three months. For three months they slept at the Fisher's every night, ate meals, left things messy, and disrupted normal family routines.

During these three months, the woman gave her life to Jesus. Clem was preaching, and a member of the congregation was translating into Czech for the three guests of the Fishers. Suddenly the woman called out and interrupted the sermon. She wanted Jesus in her heart right away! Clem led in prayer, as the woman cried out in Czech to Jesus her Lord.

Finally, the authorities found shelter for the woman and the two men. Now God opened yet another chapter for Sylvia and Clem. The first Afghans had arrived in Oberursel, including a brother and his younger sister. Both had been severely traumatized by their travel to Germany. Jesus asked Sylvia and Clem to foster parent the teenage girl. With their three sons grown and out of the house, they suddenly had a daughter in their home who was Muslim and could hardly speak German. The new relationship made for beautiful moments. It also made for many frustrating situations and painful challenges. Countless hours were spent with school authorities, in the local hospital, in the car-turned-

144

taxi, or in painful communications with an angry and traumatized teenage girl.

All of this has had a tremendous impact on Clem and Sylvia. I have watched my friends display the heart of God through their ongoing self-sacrificial use of their home, their time and their lives, I have seen them dogged with constant exhaustion, I have witnessed how they face relational challenges for which there are no apparent solutions. But the biggest impact has been on Clem and Sylvia Fisher's little congregation. The generosity and self-sacrificial nature of koinonia they exemplified jumped over on the people in the congregation.

And that is the point: the Oberursel church community of Clem and Sylvia is the one I referred to earlier as the one into which God chose to suddenly "drop" 40 Muslim Iranians one Sunday in early 2016. God knew he could entrust the Persians into a missional community, whose koinonia-love has been shaped by the koinonia-love of its founding elder and his wife. The congregation of 35 reacted immediately: they called their friends in Frankfurt-Nord and found someone who could immediately come to translate into Farsi. After the church service, they approached the many strangers personally, invited them to their homes and began to build relationships. Many of the Iranians stayed and six months later, they were able to celebrate 13 baptisms.

## Prayer:

In its "come" and in its "go" structure, the missional community becomes a community of prayer.

One of the thoughts that has comforted and motivated me time and again is that the Holy Spirit is the "Spirit of intercession" (Zechariah 12:10). The reason I find this such a comfort is that the Holy Spirit has made it his work to motivate us to pray. I do not have to take the burden on myself to convince my congregation to pray more. He who brought the Pentecostal outpouring and massive number of conversions also brings the motivation to pray for outpouring and conversions.

It appears that that is what really happened in Acts 1 and 2: Jesus announced the coming of the Holy Spirit in special power. On that basis, the 120 followers of Jesus were motivated to gather and pray. In answer to their prayers, the Holy Spirit came in the promised special power. In other words, these disciples were motivated to ask for that which Jesus had promised. In turn then, Jesus gave, what they had asked for according to his promise.

When the Holy Spirit starts to motivate, pastors do not have to manhandle believers into showing up for a prayer meeting, nor do they have to deride them for not having shown up for the prayer meeting. Just like the believers in Acts 1, when the Holy Spirit is at work pre-pentecostally, he gets believers excited about the work that God promised he will do in their midst. When those Christians then experience answers to their prayers in the form of an unusual, powerful outpouring of Pentecostal proportions, they, in turn, are motivated to ask God for more. At that point you do not have to "force" believers on their knees. They are motivated from within by the Spirit of intercession.

This translates into an important principle, as we Europeans are asking ourselves: how do we participate in a movement God has initiated? We are learning that if you notice God doing a wonderful thing in your church community—even in something small like a woman with head covering suddenly sitting in the last row—do not be quiet about it. Rejoice! Testify to God's breakthrough in your church! Tell your house churches (micro level) to give thanks to God that a Muslim woman entered the church community (at the macro level). That is a great thing! And pray to God that he will give yet another such visitor. People will feel the excitement to pray and ask for more.

We have many faithful praying people in our Mosiak churches. One couple prays every morning at 5:30 in the church center for each individual Mosaik church and its leaders.  Others meet weekly in a prayer circle to pray for the leaders and for new conversions, and once a month we spend the whole day on Saturday in prayer for the church, for the nations, and for non-believers.

When you see that God is moving here or there in your congregation, schedule something like 30 or 40 days of prayer. The American missionary, Karen Smith, scheduled daily prayer at her place for 30 days, 7:00-8:00 a.m. (on the way to work) and 6:00-7:00 p.m. (on the way home from work). Because the people had recently seen God work in miraculous ways in their congregation, they were motivated to pray. Eight to ten people showed up for each one of the prayer slots over the 30 days.

At the end of the 30 days, the worship director scheduled an entire Saturday for prayer and praise. Many people came for some time, then left. But a group of Iranians, who had recently started coming to worship services, came for the entire day. They prayed, they searched the Scriptures, they sang in their own language. One of them said he never in his life felt so much joy as on that day. What is even wilder is that the Iranians brought Syrian Muslims along. They had met them at language class a few days earlier and asked them to come along.

**Joel Lutz's Journal Entry (An elder from church #1):**

*March 27, 2016: During our prayer day yesterday, Mohammed, one of our newer refugees from Iran brought at least ten people from his German language class. They were refugees from Syria, two of which were women wearing the traditional Muslim head covering. We handed out Arabic Bibles to them and announced that the next hour was committed to reading the Psalms. Four of the Syrian men joined us for the reading. Knowing that they did not understand German or English, I quickly had to decide that we would read the Psalms in four languages (English, German, Persian, and Arabic). I asked one of the Syrian men if he would be willing to read in Arabic, and he nodded "yes". One of our Persian believers who understands a little Arabic, helped guide the Syrian man to the Psalm I had chosen for a reading. We then proceeded to read the Psalms in four languages over the next hour.*

*Afterwards, I had a chance to talk with three of the young Syrian men. Quickly I found out that they spoke English very well. Two of them told me that over the past years, their lives have been full of chaos and tragedy. Everything they lived for was completely shaken and destroyed. Then they told me that despite all of the confusion and chaos in their life, when they were in that room reading from the Bible, they felt something they never had felt before. They said they felt peace, love and gentleness. For the first time ever, they experienced something that gave them rest deep in their hearts.*

*That motivated me to share with them, that what they felt was the love of God thru His Son, Jesus. I asked them if they knew who Jesus was, and they said "yes, we know Isa and how he is a great prophet". So, I shared with them this passage from my Bible and explained that this was something that Jesus promised all of us:*

*"At that time his voice shook the earth, but now he has promised, 'Yet once more I will shake not only the earth but also the heavens.' This phrase, 'Yet once more,' indicates the removal of things that are shaken—that is, things that have been made, in order that the things that cannot be shaken may remain. Therefore, let us be grateful for receiving a kingdom that cannot be shaken, and thus let us offer to God acceptable worship, with reverence and awe."* *(Hebrews 12:26-32)*

*I explained to them that despite the fact that their world has been completely shaken, Jesus promises us His kingdom that will NOT be shaken. I shared that His kingdom is based on love and peace, and what they felt in that room was His kingdom coming to their hearts! Immediately after I said this, their faces physically shifted from complete hopelessness to hope and excitement. Then they asked, "Do you do this every week? We want to come again!!"*

## Thinking and Working Beyond Denominations:

In its "go" structure, the missional community looks beyond its denomination. Churches in Europe that are opening up their community life to people of all nations, especially to Muslims, are being swept up into God's kingdom-expansion-mission. The kingdom of God is broader than the local church: the kingship of God in people's hearts all across the globe transcends any spirit of territorialism or turf-consciousness or theological elitism.

Denominations are important. When you get swept up into God's missional movement, you take on the following kingdom mentality about your or any other denomination: "We belong to a denomination, but we don't have time to think denominationally". Ministry is not about making the name or the strategy of a local church great, it's about the kingdom of God becoming greater and greater.

When the Holy Spirit has finished his world-wide mission and Jesus suddenly returns in his glory, he is not going to ask: "Who got smart and followed the approach of this mega-church in that city? If you did not, please form a single line over here for those who receive lesser rewards". Nor will he ask, "Which denomination pushed my kingdom forward the most? Who gets the prize for greatest productivity?" One of Jesus' parables makes it clear: the workers with the least hours invested and the workers with the most hours invested all get the same prize in the end. Why? Neither of them deserved any prize at all. It was all of grace that we are allowed to serve the King of kings. The one who gets the prize for the most astounding strategy of mission in all of time is God himself.

Being trans-denominational in our mentality - some in our European context would prefer to say, 'ecumenically cooperative' - does not mean that we lower our theology to the least common denominator, nor that we write off theology as something unimportant. Theology is important, even essential. It is nothing other than "a word" (-logy) about "God" (theo-). But the only word about God any person can have is a word from God. By that I mean, all we can know about the one true God is what God has revealed to us. And he has revealed himself in person—Jesus Christ—and in writing—the Bible. To say, "I don't need theology, just give me the Bible" is foolish and naïve. The Bible is God's theology of himself and his plan of salvation throughout the ages and to every tongue, tribe and nation.

If there ever is a time for Christians to know biblical theology, it is now. Why? First of all, because our enemy's strategy at all times is to undermine the revelation of God in Jesus and through the Bible. Satan's ploy with the first couple was to call them to stand over God's word in the garden and to re-interpret it. He called the clear meaning of God's words into question: "Did God really say...?" (Genesis 3:1). That snake has not changed his strategy! He wants believers to re-interpret God's word so that they will eventually do exactly the opposite of what God has said.

Another reason why every Christian is to be prepared with robust theological answers today is that we are living in a day in which God is moving millions of people to us so that they will hear the gospel. God is sending people of all nations to our doorsteps and into our churches. Many of them are Muslims, and they are asking us theological questions: they want to know about the authority and trustworthiness of the Bible, about God as a trinity, about the divinity of Jesus, who the Holy Spirit is, and if God really can forgive their sins. This is no time to become theologically careless or dumb down our theology in order to get along with as many theological directions as possible.

Being trans-denominational in attitude, furthermore, does not mean, developing a negative attitude toward denominations. In and of themselves, denominations are good. They provide accountability for their pastors. They develop resources for ministry. They are the administrative arm that makes sure we get a pay check and operate within the laws of the land. We need to stress that in this time of spiritual-theological war all across this globe, congregations need to belong to denominations that fully grasp the need to be theologically faithful instead of theologically trendy, that provide a good balance between being theologically correct and missionally progressive, and that call their church leaders to complete conformity to biblical integrity. Where such denominations exist, we need to be thankful for and supportive of them.

What being trans-denominational does mean is that we – the local church – shape our philosophy of ministry and our gospel-driven DNA according to the mission into which God calls our local church. The denomination does not stand over the local church so as to dictate to it how to carry out its mission. The denomination allows its churches to follow God's call into mission. In other words, the denomination allows the local church to be driven by the question: 'How does our local church as a missional community reach all the unsaved people around us?' instead of being driven by the mentality: 'Are we keeping the denomination happy with us'?

Most radically of all, being trans-denominational means when God calls our local church to multiply itself into new church communities, we are willing to work cross-denominationally. In Part 1, we looked at different Mosaik church and saw that after their planting, they joined various denominations; many were willing to plant a church best led by somebody of a different denomination than their own. Or they might help a church plant in the community but of a different denomination than their own get started for the sake of the community. What binds us followers of Jesus from different denominations together as a church plant is one common goal: to get the gospel of Jesus to as many people as possible, whether they be nationals or newly-arrived refugees, not our denominational parameters.

We have created a missional community when the community is so wrapped up in God's mission that it is thankful for its denomination but does not have time to think denominationally!

?

# 10 MONO-MULTICULTURAL CONVERSIONS AND BAPTISMS

"You have something. It shines out from you, something that I have always searched for. This Jesus is the answer to my deepest questions and desires."
-    **K. from Tehran to Daniel Tischler (ICF Munich)**

One year after my 24 students, Susan and I had begun the church plant in Frankfurt, we experienced the first conversion. It was spontaneous and sudden. I had just baptized a young German in a Sunday evening worship service—one of the 24 students, who had come to faith in Jesus three years earlier; then a newborn baby of a couple that professed faith in Jesus. Suddenly I had an impulse: I called on the little congregation that was forming: "If anyone else is so inclined to give his life to Jesus' salvation and lordship right now, you can simply walk up to this bowl of water after we hear a song, and I will baptize you into faith and a life of following Jesus, even if it means they will kill you for following him."

Sure enough, after the song a young Indonesian Muslim woman came forward. She was an au pair who had come into our church planting project a few weeks earlier and had been immediately impressed with the joy of the young people. Now she stood trembling and weeping before me. She knew what her baptism would mean. Her father, a strict Muslim, had already informed her that he was disowning her for attending our church. She was about to lay her entire life on the line.

I asked her in front of the congregation why she would like to be baptized. Through the elderly Indonesian woman who translated for her, and with a quivering voice, this young woman made it clear to the congregation that if Jesus was willing to be baptized in order to identify with her unrighteousness, she wanted to be baptized in order to be identified with Jesus' righteousness. My sermon from Mark 1 about Jesus' baptism had obviously penetrated her heart. By now the girl was shaking all over. This was not cheap grace to her, this was costly. I poured water over her in the name of the Father, the Son and the Holy Spirit.

A few months later, the young woman left. She did not return to her home in Indonesia—the cost of discipleship for her was to have lost her home there. Instead, she moved to Bali. There she found a Christian church and continues to follow Jesus faithfully.

## How Quickly Should We Baptize?

Since that Sunday in 2012, the wave of refugees has grown to overwhelming proportions. And so, has the number of quick conversions and baptisms. Especially people from Muslim countries are flooding into churches, asking to be baptized. Like I did with the Indonesian lady, many pastors have moved quickly to fulfill the request for baptism. That is understandable! After years and years of decline in church attendance and after a spiritual lethargy has enveloped the European continent like a thick fog for centuries, what some churches are experiencing is a bit like Pentecost.

I fully understand the thrill of baptizing people of a non-Christian heritage into the Christian faith! One of the great examples of mass baptisms is the Dreieinigkeitskirche in Berlin. To be sure, the story of Pastor Gottfried Martens and his dying congregation is rather unique in its magnitude. Later in this book I will describe for you in greater detail how this church in Germany has exploded since 2012 through hundreds of requests from Iranians and Afghans to be baptized into the faith of Jesus. Accusations have swarmed through the air, that the Berlin pastor accedes to their requests for baptism far too quickly. But this servant of God attests to a weeks-long rigorous preparation course he puts each person through who asks to become a Christian.

Many of the refugees that are baptized are unlike the young Indonesian woman who, though baptized spontaneously, held firm in her faith to this day: Many walk away from faith in Christ and from the church not long after being baptized, revealing ulterior motives. In fact, since that first baptism, we ourselves have experienced the heart break of baptized people, both refugees and nationals, walking away from their initial profession of faith.

For that reason, we can understand the approach a pastor of a Persian church in Hamburg takes: he receives hundreds of requests for baptism by Muslims who enter his church community by directing them into a six-month long basics course. Only if the pastor discerns at the conclusion of the course that the attender's confession of faith is clear and from the heart, does he agree to baptize the person into faith in Jesus and membership of the local church. If he is not convinced that the person is willing to follow Jesus in discipleship, he tells the person to go through the course again. Many churches have taken that or a similar course of action.

## Pro or Anti: "quick baptism"

Baptize immediately or after a learning-and-testing-period? We do well to take a step back for a moment, and consider the theology and arguments for both approaches:

**Arguments for quick baptism usually run like this:**

- Since only God can see into the heart, it is not ours to judge the authenticity of someone's claim to be, or want to be, a Christian.
- Baptism is not merely a symbol of what has happened spiritually in a person's heart, it is a seal of the salvation God is granting the person. To withhold baptism amounts to withholding from the person a means whereby he may be assured that God has fully accepted him into God's grace.
- Baptism includes and implants the seed of regeneration. When a person is baptized, even a baby, he is deeply and authentically united to Christ. I myself do not believe that baptism implants a seed of regeneration, but opponents of that view need to consider that the apostle Peter did write, "baptism now saves you" (1 Peter 3:21).

**Arguments for the need to see evidence of genuine conversion before baptism run like this:**

- There simply are too many people who walk away from the faith not long after their supposed conversion, making a mockery of their confession of faith and of the church. I myself believe that proponents of this view need to consider what Jesus taught us regarding the weeds (Matthew 13:36-43). It is not for us to pull up the weeds now, lest we mistakenly pull up good wheat. Jesus will pull up the weeds at the judgment on the last day.
- It is true that only God can know what really is in the heart. But God also expects Christians to discern from people's actions, if they are obediently following Jesus. That is why Peter could judge Simon the Sorcerer, who had joined the apostles and new believers, and say "your heart is not right with God" (Acts 8:21). The

meaning of Matthew 7:1, "judge not, lest you be judged" does not mean that a person's lifestyle is not under accountability to the body of Christ, nor does it contradict that we are to admonish people who call themselves followers of Jesus but according to Scripture live unrepentantly in a lifestyle of sin.

- If we baptize adults who say they want to be Christians, but actually want nothing more than a certificate that states they belong to the church, we give them a false assurance of salvation.

## Let's consider some Biblical points about conversion:

What does a true conversion consist of? Let's look at several biblical points that are relevant to the question of baptism:

## First, Conversion is not changing from one religion to another religion.

It is being driven by the gospel to Jesus as personal Savior and Lord. Belief in Christ is not a religion in its truest sense. All religions operate out of a deeply ingrained mindset that faith in God is tantamount to following a list of rules. A good Muslim follows all of them faithfully all the time, a bad Muslim follows them better the older he gets and the more seriously he takes the five pillars of Islam. When he enters a Christian church, the average Muslim is looking for a clear Christian codex. When he says he wishes to convert to Christianity, he might be merely saying that he would like to know what that Christian code of conduct is that replaces the Islamic set of rules. Conversion means to him exchanging one list of rules for another.

To be sure, Christianity includes a clear set of morals. It has its Ten Commandments. It involves a lifestyle of biblical ethics that reflects the holiness of God. But Christianity—and for that matter, conversion to Christ—does not begin with a moral code. It begins with the law of God that tells me "in and of myself I am more sinful than I ever dared to believe". Having convinced my heart that I am utterly unable to do anything to secure God's acceptance, the gospel then points me to the cross and pronounces: "but in Christ I am more loved than I ever dared to hope."

The gospel and religion are diametrically opposed. Here are three ways that is true:

- **Religion says:** I am as good as the works I achieve for God.
  **The Gospel says:** Jesus performed the perfect work for God in my place.

**Conclusion:** Perfection is no longer a standard for how good I must be to be acceptable to God. The cross fulfilled that standard.

- **Religion says:** I am as significant as I am desirable to others.
  **The Gospel says:** In Christ God finds me passionately desirable and longs to be mine.

**Conclusion:** Desirability is no longer a standard for my significance or acceptance. The cross fulfilled that standard.

- **Religion says:** I am safe and secure as long as the people important to me remain faithful to me.
  **The Gospel says:** Jesus was forsaken by God in my place, so that God will never have a reason to forsake me.

**Conclusion:** Whether or not others remain faithful to me is no longer a guarantee of my security. The cross has fulfilled that standard.

The point is that the gospel cuts through all religious thinking. God has given us the gospel of Jesus in order to free us from all self-imposed standards and to liberate our significance and security from how others treat us. In talking about conversion, nothing is more essential than to recognize that salvation is not a change from one religion to another religion. It is embracing the gospel, that Jesus has done everything and is everything for me.

**The second biblical point is that conversion is much more than a decision we make in the mind. It involves the whole person.**

Discipleship involves the whole person and every aspect of the person. Jesus commissioned us to go and make disciples of all nations, "teaching them to obey whatsoever I (Jesus) have commanded you" (Matthew 28:20). In Jesus' mind, obeying him is a synonym for loving him (John 14:23-24). On the surface, obedience is a decision the believer makes with his will. He decides to do something he wasn't doing, or to stop doing something he was doing. But the will does not float around freely in our being. It is connected to the affections, to what we love, to our desires and passions. These drive our will; they inform the will what they would like the will to will.

But just like the will, the desires are also not disconnected from the rest of our being. They arise out of the attitudes we have. If we have a negative attitude about something, our desire will be to avoid it, flee from it, beat it and destroy it, or to push it out of our memory. If we have a positive attitude about something, we will want to move toward it, grasp hold of it, experience it, praise it, and pass it on to others. What determines whether we have a positive or negative attitude about something is the interpretation we have given to it. We interpret events, people, institutions and experiences as positive or negative based on the values we assign to them. Again, these assigned values have roots that go deep into the core of our being: our underlying belief system or world view we have developed. This belief system consists of what we believe about God, about self, about the world around us, about life and about life after death. Again, what determines our belief system is—and here we come back to what I mentioned in the first point—the inclination of our human nature, or what the Bible calls "heart".

I hope you were able to track all the connections with me.

- Obedience (Lifestyle)
- Will (Decisions)
- Affections (Passions)
- Attitude (Disposition)
- Interpretation (Mental Processing)
- Belief (Faith)
- Inclination (Heart; Human nature)

The point is that obedience is not merely an outward act. It is the end result of all aspects of our humanness all linked together. Starting with the deepest core, the heart, and moving all the way to the visible actions, the question is: Is Jesus Lord? True regeneration by the Holy Spirit leads a person to submit to the lordship of Jesus in every aspect of his being.

## Another Biblical truth is that genuine conversion can only be recognized over time by its fruit.

This follows from our first two points and is underscored by Jesus himself in the most poignant judgment he delivered: "Not everyone who says to me, 'Lord, Lord' will enter the kingdom of heaven" (Matthew 7:21). The double expression of 'Lord' purports a very pious stance of the person. You might experience this person as someone who regularly attends worship services and accords God the highest praise. Jesus' words are like razor blades cutting into muscle and tissue.

He says, that these "double-Lord-worshippers" will appear before Jesus at the final judgment, and they will point to miraculous acts they did and great powers they had over demons. But Jesus will say to them, "Get away from me! I never knew you!" (Matthew 7:23).

On another occasion, Jesus made a severe analysis of faith with the picture of the sower and the seed. In Matthew 13:21, Jesus likens a certain person in whom the seed of the gospel was sown, as having "received" the gospel into his life "with great joy". Later, however, he falls away from the faith, because his longing for certain things in life overwhelms and chokes any faith he might have had. The apostle Paul called it sailing your ship of faith against a rock and shipwrecking (1 Timothy 1:18).

The scripture wants to warn us of self-deception. You might think you are on your way to heaven, but in actuality are lost and on your way to hell. If your faith is not a gift from the Spirit (John 3:6; Ephesians 2:8-9) but something you produced yourself, it is only a matter of time before you turn into a Judas, who followed Jesus as one of the 12 charter members of the new covenant church, then threw it all away: he decided he preferred to have Jesus nailed to a cross and exposed as a fool than to be a fool who takes up his cross and follows Jesus.

Sometimes, what is really in a person's heart is revealed only when he falls into hard times or works through his first disappointments with God.

**Finally, we must remember the great news about conversion: it can happen in the most unusual of ways:**

The Gospels and the book of Acts are replete with people experiencing unusual encounters with the supernatural. Of course, there are differing views about how we should view the miracles described there. There are those who believe that God works miracles all the time; that spiritual gifts that are of a more spectacular nature are given to the church all the time, like the gifts of miracles, healing, and discerning evil spirits. On the other hand, there are interpreters of God's Word who see unusual encounters with the supernatural—as described in the Gospels and in Acts—as well as the accompanying spectacular gifts, as highly unusual and not to be expected today.

Whichever of these two views you hold, there is no question that great miracles are occurring and that we are in a special time of history. Reports are coming in from the Mid-East, from Asia, from Africa, that many astonishing kinds of conversions are taking place. Just like in the Middle East, Muslims in our cities are having dreams in which Jesus appears to them.

The first man in the initial Mosaik congregation to encounter Jesus in a dream was an Afghan man. Thirteen hours after the dream he came to our worship service. He told us that he saw a bright light walk into his room during the night. From the waist down, the light looked like a man, and from the waist up it was like the magnificent sun. It was Jesus, and Jesus laid his hand on the Afghan's right shoulder and told him to come to our church a few hours later. Convinced of the reality of the risen Lord, that man gave his life to Jesus a few Sundays later.

Another Muslim spoke of having a dream in which he was eagerly searching for the truth. When he heard a noise behind him he turned around and saw Jesus standing with his arms outstretched and saying to him: "I am the way, the truth and the life." When he told someone in our congregation about this dream, the person took him to John 14:6 and showed him that Jesus had actually said these words 2000 years ago. That man gave his life to Jesus.

A Pakistani man, a great Mullah, had gone to Greece as a Muslim missionary. He was convinced he needed to follow the Koran and force Greeks to either pay taxes to the mosque or be killed if they did not repent and convert to Islam. One night he had a dream that he was walking down a street and suddenly noticed brilliant light exploding through a store window and out onto the street. He felt a longing to

161

understand that light, so he went toward it. When he arrived at the store, he was drawn by the light into the store. He entered and saw that the entire store was filled with beautiful, shining vessels. Behind the counter stood a man who was the source of the tremendous beam of light. "It is all yours," he said to the Muslim. "I purchased it all for you. You can have the whole store." The Pakistani man answered: "But I am not worthy to own these beautiful pieces." Jesus answered: "You do not have to be worthy. I paid for it all, and I want to give it to you as a gift."

Just then the dream was interrupted. The two men who had been sleeping in the same room woke him up. "What do you want?" the Muslim imam asked his two companions. One of them said, "What do you mean 'What do you want'? Did you not see it? The whole room was full of light. Do you know where it came from?" That Mullah gave his life to Jesus a few weeks later.

Healings are also occurring, in ways we had never before experienced. A team in the pediatric practice of Dr. Behr prayed for a baby from Kosovo, when after six months the doctors couldn't find a reason for her continual fevers. The fever left immediately, and her happy mother entrusted her life to Jesus in the following days.

In many places in Europe, especially where North African and Middle Eastern refugees are pouring into churches, there are accounts of miraculous occurrences and amazing conversions like the ones I described. For a pastor to tell the Hindu man "No, go back to your seat, you must be baptized before you take the Lord's Supper", or to a Syrian woman to whom Jesus appeared in a dream, "I need six months to determine if you are sincere in your desire to follow Jesus", seems hard and inflexible. It would be like the Ethiopian man in Acts 8, sitting on his horse-drawn-wagon, and reading a scroll of Isaiah 53. God had put Philipp the evangelist into the desert and into the path of the wagon, in order to explain to the African what Isaiah 53 means. The Ethiopian was so quickly stirred by the gospel that in seeing a body of water, asked: "Is there anything that should prevent me from being baptized?" (Acts 8:37). Imagine, if Philipp had answered: "Well yes, actually. We need to test this conversion of yours, because there is no way to know if you are being real about this or not. Time will tell if it is genuine. How about we meet next year, same time same place, and if you have remained true, I will baptize you." Nothing of the sort! Philipp took the man down into the water and baptized him immediately.

There is no formula by which to answer the question, how close to one's conversion he should be baptized. There are many people who are being dramatically converted to Jesus from one moment to the next. There are also people who are asking to be baptized because they have come to hate the religion they grew up in and want to change to a new religion. And there are people who hope that a certificate of baptism from a church in their new home will heighten their chances of being accepted into Western society. We need wisdom.

On the one hand, if we baptize people because they simply want the label "Christian" stuck to their name, we are adding to the plague that has beset our church for several hundreds of years already: a cultural or nominal Christianity that is confused as true Christianity. What is worse, we give them a false assurance of salvation and contribute to the destruction of their own souls.

On the other hand, there are many real conversions happening. God seems to be "going out of his way" to move people to places where they hear the gospel and quickly turn to Jesus for salvation. To refuse these people baptism is to become a hindrance to the Spirit's work in their lives. It is to withhold from them the very seal that God uses to mark a person's conversion and minister to him assurance of having been truly accepted by the Lord.

My recommendations, therefore, are:

- If you, like Philipp the evangelist, witnessed the conversion of a person, and it is clear to you that the "converting" one had a real encounter with the Lord, do not delay the baptism. However, baptize the person with the agreement that the new believer will immediately move into your "Basic Christianity" class to be discipled in his new faith.

- If you are approached by someone you do not know, and no one else in the congregation knows the person, and he asks you to baptize him, direct the person into a "Basic Christianity" course. Here are a few recommendations for such a course:
  - o Design a course that functions rotationally, that anybody can enter at any time.
  - o It needs to be tailored to the person's background: use one kind of "baptism-preparation-class" for someone converting from Islam, and another kind of course for someone with a secular, atheistic background.
  - o Make the course intense. Give homework. Have people do practical exercises, like sharing their faith with someone who will not kill them for it.
  - o Cover the bases in your course, especially the controversial themes: the identity of Jesus, what the Bible says about its own authority, about God the Trinity, sin, the radical nature of conversion and discipleship, Satan, the cross and resurrection, the church, the meaning of Pentecost, end times and the place of Israel in history (since this is a stumbling block for many Muslims), spiritual warfare, facing temptations, personal holiness and obedience, developing your character as a Spirit-filled believer, how to read the Bible, how to make prayer into a lifestyle, how to place your sexuality under the Lordship of Jesus and the authority of his Word, how to

share your faith with others, how to recognize and use your spiritual gifts in the church. And, of course, they need to know the meaning of baptism, as well as what happens in the Lord's Supper.

If, in the end, the person who was unknown to you indicates that he not only accepts the salvation but the lordship of Jesus over every aspect of his being, baptize the person.

- If you are approached by a person for baptism, and in asking the person why he desires the mark of belonging to Jesus, he tells you he would like to belong to the church or be accepted by the government, you certainly do not want to baptize that person. You most definitely will direct him into the "Basic Christianity" course, in the hope that during the course the Holy Spirit will open his heart to genuinely become a follower of Jesus.

## Celebrating Baptism

When you baptize newly converted people, make it a festive occasion. Celebrate afterwards with a meal together. If possible, baptize several at once. Some people are satisfied with being sprinkled. Many like to be baptized by going fully under water. If your sanctuary does not have a baptismal pool, I recommend two options:

- In the warm weather, you can celebrate a special baptismal service at a river or lake nearby and have the congregation gather there. If it is so cold that the river or lake is frozen over, do not try to punch a hole into the ice. Look for a church building that has a baptismal pool and rent it for a special service.

- Another option is to do what Georg did: he wanted to be baptized by immersion in a sanctuary that had no baptismal tank. I knew that I had to be away at a conference the entire week leading up to Georg's baptism, so I simply encouraged him to organize something: "You are in charge of securing your own baptismal tank. Go get something that works, and I will reimburse you for it. Whatever it is, when I get here on Sunday, have it set up and full of water." When I arrived for the worship service, Georg was dressed in a white robe. I greeted him cheerfully, then looked around worried: "Oh no, there is no baptismal tank!" Georg smiled: "it's out in the parking lot. I want to be baptized out under the sun. I got a little baby pool. We blew it up and filled it with water before you came." I laughed. "Why a children's pool?" Georg's answer was ingenious, I thought: "It's easy to carry, easy to set up, easy to fill. Besides that, I am supposed to have faith like a child. What better way to express that than to be baptized in a baby pool!" About 20 Turks showed up for the service, all of whom were friends of Georg. It was the craziest baptism I ever experienced, because nobody besides me knew what was "proper protocol" for baptism. At the end of the service, we all walked out onto the parking lot. Georg's friends stood as close to the pool as possible. Four of them immediately lit up cigarettes. As I stepped into the water and opened my mouth to begin my explanation, cigarette smoke wafted into my face.

Since that memorable baptism, we use the baby pool for every baptism. But we now have a sign hanging on the front of the pool that reads: "No

Smoking".

# 11 FACING OUR FEARS

"Multi-culti is not nice at all. These foreigners receive our money thrown at them by the government, they take our women and our work...I've had it up to here."

**Thorsten, from the book *Warum wir das Schaffen Müssen***

## There is Much Fear

In Germany, fear is taking hold. What have we done by taking in all of these refugees? Is it naïve simply to move forward with the welcome-culture? Can we really do it, as Angela Merkel never tires of saying? Or are PEGIDA (Patriotic Europeans Against the Islamification of the Occident) and AfD (Alternative for Germany) right, that we are destroying our Christian heritage? German society is deeply divided over these questions. Already there has been a significant increase in the number of crimes against refugees, Since the flood of refugees in the fall of 2015, the questions within the German people have also grown. In other countries, the fences were built higher. While I was working on this book, in December 2016, the attack at the Christmas market in Berlin occurred.

Many Christians also swing back and forth between mercy for the suffering people, who pulled together their last resources to make the dangerous journey to Europe, and the concern over the invasion and impact of a culture and a religion that is so different from that of our western culture. For many, this concern has grown into a deep-seated fear.

## Fear is Not Always Justified

Fear is not a good motivator, as the expression goes. Sometimes fear is a psychological reaction to something that reminds us of something bad that happened to us in the past. For example, years ago, when my friend's big dog laid his head on my lap, I immediately felt fear and the sweat drops on my head: the dog looked exactly like the beast that had torn into me with bared teeth when I was seven years old. Of course, "there was no cause for fear" because it was not the same dog. But I associated the dog with my little trauma as a child.

In the same way many people carry traumatic experiences with foreigners around with them, for example, because they were grabbed once in the subway, or because their families suffered in East Germany under the Russian occupiers.

There are many things that can cause us fear when so many people of different cultures and world views and values step onto our turf! The arrival of hundreds of thousands of strangers on our doorstep reminds me of Psalm 53:6, "They were afraid when there was no cause to be afraid!"

Fear can also be a weapon of Satan to keep us from obediently following Jesus. We do not say things, do things, or go places because we are afraid of what might happen or of how people might react. Of course, we really do not know what will happen or if people will actually turn on us. We simply imagine the worst. But if we could see into the future, we would see how God holds us in his hand and that "there was no cause for fear".

Fear can be caused by our lack of faith in God's sovereign control of our lives. A lack of faith means a lack of seeing God in the situation. You may feel the need to control every situation and circumstance: you want things to develop according to your standard, to happen within your comfort zone, and to turn out according to your expectations. Too little faith means you do not see God in the situation, only your own ability to control that situation. But when you walk by faith and not by sight (2 Corinthians 5:7), you see God's large fingers wrapped around your tiny person, directing every step you take, protecting you from anything that could destroy you (Romans 8:28), and turning your steps in the direction of victory (Romans 8:38-39). When you have much faith, you will move into the situation in which God is calling you to serve and witness, leaving the consequences to him. Faith informs you that in the hand of a sovereign God, there is "no cause for fear."

The flood of refugees upon our continent has raised many fears. We would do well to evaluate these fears and to ask ourselves if there really is cause for fear:

## Fear #1: "I fear we will lose our economic wellbeing"

Statistics at the beginning of 2016 show that the economy in the country that has taken in by far the most refugees—Germany—has not suffered economically at all from the wave of new people and their many needs. Surprisingly, it has improved. Germany has an aging population with thousands of open job opportunities; this could be a chance for a demographic development. Added to that, we are receiving hundreds of thousands of children, who will grow up to be 1.5 or 2.0 generation adults. They could help make up for the downward economic spiral that is predicted due to nationals not having enough children to keep the nation's economy going. It is no surprise to hear economists' predictions of a direct link between the arrival of a few million refugees and an economic upsurge.

But let's go behind this fear! What if we were to take an economic beating? As one of the richest countries in the world, we may be thankful to God that he has given us many years of economic blessing. It is God's grace alone that the country has been blessed so richly. "Grace" means a gift that is not deserved. Anytime a country enjoys economic wellbeing as an undeserved gift from God, the Giver of every good gift and the Owner of every Euro, it owes God public thanksgiving. Sure, we can point to our commitment to hard work and industriousness, or to our high intelligence and educational system, as the reason for our wellbeing. Politicians do it all the time. The greater tragedy is when followers of Jesus drift into the secularist mentality and turn our careers, bank accounts, academic credentials or comfortable homes into evidence of importance and accomplishment, and into sources of security, joy, and a sense of wellbeing.

The wave of refugees is no cause for fear that we will lose our economic wellbeing. Instead, the foreigners give us opportunity to express to them the best in life: not great careers and titles and wealth, but mercy, kindness, love and justice.

## Fear #2: "I fear all these new cultures will change our country's culture."

This particular fear is stated often by good citizens and deserves some consideration. Hardly anyone doubts that in many places, especially in cities, the majority of the residents are no longer the nationals but the immigrants who have moved there. When one child in the kindergarten is the only German-background, non-Muslim child, or the teacher isn't respected by her Turkish students because they have learned at home that women have nothing to say to them, then it's possible to feel like a stranger in your own country. And when Thilo Sarrazin, in his book, Deutschland schafft sich ab (2010), describes his perception that Germany is destroying itself and its values through the arrival of lazy, uneducated Muslims who take advantage of the social system, then we can understand why there is a growing fear that we are losing the German culture.

The fact is, every country in the world experiences a change in culture. "Culture", simply put, has to do with how we live life, and cope with change—how we manage our existence. And every culture is in flux all the time. Take your own country: today's culture is very different from what it was 40 years ago. Why? Because of immigrants? No! Because people change, generations change, new things are invented, technological progress is made. Consequently, new things, faster things, and more things are expected. Cultures shift with the shifting of people, their mentality and worldview. Many of the deep fears of people who join the AfD oder PEGIDA, actually stem from globalization; these challenges would be happening even when no immigrants were streaming into our country.

The change-trend of cultures generally flows from restriction to a liberalization of ethics. Look at the trend just in the past 60 years: what was considered by all as murder was eventually legalized as abortion; what was considered in the West as a psychological abnormality is legalized as homosexual marriage; what was commonly viewed by our grandparents as complete debauchery—a man and woman moving in together and having sex without being married—is accepted today as normal, everyone's right and, in fact, a beneficial, low-risk way to try out a relationship.

Regardless of where you stand on these issues, the ethical trend in Western culture is rarely from liberalized to conservative, from "yes" to "no", or from "allowed" to "forbidden" but the other way around. And regardless of whether you think that is good or bad, the fact is that it is that way. Culture is always changing, because good citizens of a country push the lines that have been drawn to the limit and then beyond. Most of us "learned" that behavior as little kids! In fact, if you feel more committed to conservative values, you may have more in common with many of the Muslims than with your own culture, since they share many of the Christian ethics, such as a high value of the family, marriage between a man and a woman, the value of the unborn child, and values related to relationships and community.

But what lies behind this fear of our culture changing? It is a longing for security. We don't want our culture to change because we feel secure in a situation we know we can handle. As Christians, we know we live in a changing culture. We know that as we can find much good in our (and every) culture, there is evil, and the trend usually is to change the good to evil and call it "good". It is at this point that the Christian recalls himself to the fact that his permanent citizenship is "in heaven" (Philippians 3:21) and that his calling from the King of heaven is to live in our Babylons on earth, not sheltered from cultural changes or evil trends, but seeking "the welfare (Shalom) of the city where I have sent you into exile, and pray to the Lord on its behalf; for in its welfare (Shalom) you will have welfare (Shalom)" (Jeremiah 29:7).

## Fear #3: "I fear Islam, what it could do to our nation, and the safety of our children."

Are we being run over by Muslims? Many Germans feel that is currently the case, but the numbers show us something different. While Germans in a survey at the end of 2016 estimated the percentage of all Muslims in Germany at about 20%, the BAMF (Bundesamt für Migration und Flüchtlinge) counted 4.5 million Muslim residents in Germany. That represents just a quarter of the number guessed at by the German population, just over 5% of the population, hardly a major invasion.

But what is with the tendency towards violence? To bring clarity to the theme "Violence and Terrorism", we need to distinguish between Islam and Muslims. Many Muslims do not live out the Islamic religion in the way that the Koran teaches; in Islam there are just as many liberal tendencies as in Christianity.

The fact is, Islam is not just a religion but a social order. Its convictions extend over the formation of a lifestyle and culture, reaching into every area of life. Muslims are simply the people who live in this culture and religion. The teachings of Islam give them the standards by which they build their families, work, relationships and politics. They bring this lifestyle with them into their host countries, but when they step into our culture, they also start to experience a cultural change. This change, of course, happens differently depending on how ready each individual is and how deeply each person finds their own identity in the old culture of their homeland.

We must also distinguish between the various streams of Islam. There isn't just one type of Islam, but a number of divisions. The two main divisions in Islam (similar to our Catholic and Protestant confessions) are the Shia and the Sunni. Furthermore, Shia Islam is split into various branches (like denominations), and together they make up about 15 percent of the world's Muslims. What distinguishes the Shia from the Sunni is the issue of successor, the question, "Through whom was true Islam passed on to us after the final prophet, Mohammed?"

Shia Muslims are adamant that true Islam passed through Mohammed's bloodline. When Mohammed died, his male next of kin, namely Ali (Ibn Ali Talib), rightly wore the mantle of Islamic leadership. But here's the problem: Mohammed had not elected Ali as his successor. Consequently, many Muslims elected Abu Bakr as the first Khalifa after Mohammed's death. From this group the Sunni Muslims developed. They make up about 80 percent of all Muslims in the world, and they, too, have different schools of thought on various issues.

The remaining Muslims are either Ahmadiyya or Alevi Muslims. The Adhmadiyya Muslims were founded by Mirza Ghulam Ahmad at the end of the nineteenth century and have built a separate society, which, although built on the five pillars of Islam, also follows the revelation of its founder and is viewed by the Sunni and Shia Muslims as a sect. The Alevi Muslims are primarily in Turkey and Syria and follow Ali (like the Shia Muslims), but do not have mosques, but rather prayer houses, and are generally more liberal.

In addition to these theological distinctives of Islam, there is also the "volks islam", which is found throughout worldwide Islam and which has strong ties to the occult. The majority of Muslims believe on angels, spirits, the devil, holy signs, holy places, damnation for sin, wonders and the meaning of dreams as a guide in life. My colleague, Heiko Wenzel, explained to me that the strong belief in the mystical, the intrusion of the supernatural into the life of a Muslim, is an important reason why churches and Christians with more openness for visions, healing and appearances of Jesus are able to reach Muslims better than those churches and Christians who shy away from wonders, healings and surprising interventions of God. In contrast, churches that open themselves to Muslims experience things that we can only explain as God's surprising intervention (see Chapter 10).

Within these various streams of Islam, there is a deep-seated hatred, especially between the Sunni Muslims and the others. This is related to the theme of violence that affects Europeans so deeply. Sunni Muslims interpret the Koran to demand the death of all unbelievers, including Muslims who are not Sunnis. In the Koran, there are various statements related to this command. Many verses specifically command that unbelievers should be killed, while others call on the believers to treat unbelievers with love.

Why do the Sunnis place so much weight on the violent passages of the Koran, while others emphasize the verses calling them to peace and tolerance? The answer lies in Mohammed himself. Muslims believe that they should follow the example of Mohammed, as it is outlined in the Koran. The problem is that Mohammed was not always consistent: when he himself was persecuted in Mecca, he was tolerant towards his enemies. But later when he was living in Medina and could fully practice his faith, he grabbed his sword and led wars against all unbelievers. Sunnis believe that Mohammed's later stage of life has more authority than the earlier stage, so true Muslims should be intolerant of unbelievers. The other three streams of Muslims focus on Mohammed's earlier stage of life. For this reason, Islam is a religion of peace for them.

Should Europeans fear that Muslims will bring danger to our lives? We should recognize that most of the Muslims who are coming to Europe were themselves persecuted by Sunnis and believe in the peaceful view of Islam. There will always be Sunni-influenced Muslims who allow themselves to be trained as terrorists and come with this viewpoint to

Europe—or those who grow up in Europe and then go to Afghanistan or Syria to be trained as terrorists. But by and large, we can view the Muslims coming to Europe as peace-loving people who are seeking a peaceful life.

Most of the people coming as refugees to Europe are fleeing very difficult situations. Especially refugees from Somalia or Eritrea have hardly experienced anything other than war. Many have been traumatized by violence in their homelands and, in addition, have experienced unbelievable tragedies during their flight to Europe (see Chapter 3). In tense situations in this foreign place, they may react with violence, not because of their religion, but because they haven't learned anything else. This is also true of some violent Europeans.

The last and deepest reason why we can approach this wave of refugees without fear is the reason I already mentioned regarding the fear of losing our cultural identity: we, who belong to God, have a homeland not here on earth, but are citizens of heaven. Our greatest comfort in life and in death is that we "belong not to ourselves but to Jesus, our Redeemer" (Heidelberg Catechism, 1563; Question 1). We recognize that Jesus holds us at all times in his hand, and that we will someday be in his presence. This belief fills us while we are on earth with peace and freedom, confidence and conviction.

## Fear #4: "I fear what all these new people will do to my church."

Rightly so! The influx of people from different cultures into our mono-cultural churches will definitely change our congregations. But maybe that is a good thing! Pastors report how their worship services have become more chaotic and emotional. Their people complain about the noise that results from the murmuring of the translators. One reports that the wave of refugees has so steamrolled over his church that none of their normal events take place anymore: "No one has time for elders' meetings, even the youth group doesn't happen at it normal time because of a lack of helpers" says one pastor. "People are volunteering to serve the refugees every which way. We are experiencing a once-in-a-lifetime opportunity, because Muslims are coming into the church., experiencing such love, that out of thankfulness, they are coming to faith in Jesus."

Take for example the Mosaik project #3 in Oberursel, which has experienced similar things. This was a small group of about 35 people. As suddenly 40 Muslim Iranians invaded the worship service one Sunday, everything was disrupted. People who had sat in the same chair for 20 years were displaced, some even had to sit on the floor. All of a sudden, they needed translators, and they couldn't make the noisy kids understand that they should be quiet. The cake after the service was eaten away by the strange men before the church members could even get close to it. But in the next months, a number of these Iranians had become believers in Jesus. And as one of them sang a song he had composed in Farsi about God's grace and Jesus as his Redeemer during a worship service, a number of the long-time members cried tears of joy.

A pastor from Karlsruhe, Germany underscored for me the fact that there is no way an invasion of refugees into a local congregation will keep the culture and the identity of that congregation untouched. He heard one of his own elders complain loudly to several members of the congregation: "Since these refugees have come into our church, we are 'überfremdet'" (literally 'overstranged'), by which he meant that strangers have come like a wave over the nationals of that church. The pastor explained to several of us how deeply convicted he felt by that outburst in that moment. "I thought about the church; how Jesus is the head of the church and as such has the absolute right to decide who is in his church; how his Spirit even places people into local churches according to how their spiritual gifts fit best with everybody else's spiritual gifts (1 Corinthians 12:18), and how we usurp his headship and make it our own, and we grasp hold of the authority he has to place people into congregations, as if we were the head of the church and we had the authority to decide who may be in our local church and who may not."

The pastor met with his elder team and shared with them how that comment by one of their own uncovered for him the idolatry and pride of his own heart. All the elders were convicted. They prayed together, and the Lord spoke to them that he wanted them to let go of deciding who was welcome in the church community and who was not. God wanted to decide himself how he wanted to use them as a church. They were purchased at a high price; they should do his will and let themselves be led by him, as God wanted to lead them.

Within three years their church had completely changed: the formerly white, German congregation grew tremendously and was now made up of two-thirds non-Germans. The pastor remarked: "We have experienced many conversions. Everybody is excited about God's powerful work in our midst. Especially the Germans!"

Our churches are not our own. And that's good, because through the many immigrants, especially from the Near and Mid-East areas, God is bringing the western church back to that which was the church in the New Testament. Of course, I don't mean by that that we need to give up our biblical, historical theology so that we can concentrate on the lowest common denominator and become a church that tolerates everything and believes in nothing. In fact, it's is the opposite: Muslims believe in absolute truth and will never interest themselves in a church that denies absolute truth. Instead, they will be fascinated by a church that incarnates the absolute truth of the person of Jesus Christ.

When we leave it to Jesus to design the make-up of our congregation, while we concentrate on being obedient to his missional mandate, we are opening ourselves up to a big adventure. The alternative is pride and idolatry.

What I mean is that the values of the New Testament, such as hospitality, fellowship and a public faith, that have been lost in our western culture and even in our churches, are often lived out by Muslims. Is it possible that God is sending Muslims into our churches, to bring new life into these Christian values that we have lost? Should we open our churches to immigrants so that we can experience what I called the boomerang-effect in Chapter 6?

I think so! Here are a few examples for these biblical values from earlier Christianity:

- **The home and hospitality:** Most non-western cultures, including Middle Eastern and North African cultures, place a tremendous emphasis on the home as a place of peace and belonging. This is why Muslim cultures expect that visitors – be they friends or strangers, be the visits planned or spontaneous – be received into one's home, be treated with kindness, and be provided with food in generous portions. A good host is even willing to go hungry if that is what it takes for the guest to go away filled. Culture groups that bring this emphasis on home and hospitality into our fast-paced society that knows of fast-food, locked doors and a retreat into one's private corner after a high-stress day, can only do us good. In fact, they are only a step away from the New Testament teaching, that home and hospitality is more than one's love for cooking or entertaining: it is a concrete way to express the hospitality of God, who invites us into the home of his heart and nourishes us with his grace until we are satiated, even at his own expense.

- **Community:** Muslims do everything in groups. Fellowship with one another is essential to quality of life. They love to sit together, eat together, go to church together, leave church together, discuss heatedly together. They are a together-culture. The collective takes priority over the individualistic. This is why liturgical elements in a worship service, where we all together read or pray or confess together with one voice, is attractive to Oriental or African cultures. People from societies that live in connectivity and collectivity can help the church of the West return to the deep community spirit lived out by the mother church in Jerusalem (Acts 2,42-47).

- **Public Faith:** For Muslims, it is completely normal to speak about God in public. They do not make a distinction between secular and sacred things. This mentality collides with our banning of the faith into the sphere of private life. Muslims in our communities will challenge us to move our faith out of our private comfort-zones and to talk about the Healer of the World with people wherever we are.

## Overcoming the Fears

The flood of so many refugees and immigrants will definitely bring lots of changes with it. But do we need to be afraid? Can we not see the opportunity in this situation, to trust God and allow him to lead his church the way HE wants to?

Let's look again at what Pastor Gottfried Martens from the Trinity Church in Berlin-Steglitz experienced, as he—against all the fears—welcomed refugees into his fully normal church. In 2008, this brave Lutheran church consisted of ten active members, all over 70 years of age. At that time, they were not just talking about closing the church, but tearing down the hundred-year-old building. But God obviously had different plans, since in this year suddenly two Iranians appeared at the door and asked to be baptized because they wanted to become Christians. Martens fulfilled their wish, and the two invited other Iranians. Three years after, other individual Iranians were giving their lives to Jesus. Then in 2012, from this little snowball developed an avalanche; the church grew steadily so that today there are 900 members. Three-fourths of them are not German and have found their way to Jesus in these past years.

There are neighborhood residents who are irritated by the development. In 2014, residents started attempting to place hindrances on the work of the church, because they saw this invasion of refugees as a threat to their neighborhood. First, they complained to the government about the many events taking place at the church. Then they complained about the noise level (because suddenly every Sunday morning the organ was playing) and demanded financial compensation; the church agreed to keep its windows closed during the church services, even on hot days. When the church put on an annual children's festival and built tents on the property for the festival, the neighbors went to the city government because they were afraid that the church was planning to build a refugee camp.

But Pastor Martens stuck with it, even though the work often brought him to the edge of exhaustion. He emphasizes that the welcoming of refugees dramatically changed his church. But the changes don't consist only of annoyance and exhaustion, constant chaos and the feeling of being out of control. Today there are 900 people in the worship services, instead of ten old people, and the church is full of young adults. Instead of an hour long, the church service is three hours long and is no longer so exactly planned as before, but rather a lively mix of liturgical and spontaneous elements. Formerly there were major discussions about mundane things like the paint colors; now the members meet to discuss ways to fulfill their calling of integrating people from other lands into the church.

A spirit of harmony, that Martens can only view as supernatural, rules the church. This is especially evident after the church service as the people eat together. There are many hearty conversations, and everyone participates. The spiritual life of the church has also attracted many Germans in the meantime. Even from the neighborhood, people have found their way into the church and into faith in Jesus, because they were so fascinated by the faith and the lifestyles of these people from other cultures. Martens emphasizes that believers in Germany can learn a lot from persecuted Christians and their radical seriousness in faith. Their joy that they express over so many aspects of the gospel to which we have become accustomed can also changes our lives for the good.

Let's take courage to overcome our fears! It will take us on an adventure.

# 12 FROM FRUSTRATION TO FULLFILLMENT

"Nothing is more fulfilling than to experience how people from countries that are closed to the gospel come to a living faith in Christ in our midst."

**- A coworker**

## Honesty

"Lies...Lies...Lies! They just speak one lie after another," a very frustrated co-worker complained to me bitterly. She echoed the frustration of many other relief workers. In addition to the fears addressed in the former chapter, there is a whole list of stumbling blocks that make the work with refugees and immigrants difficult. Whoever wants to build a mono-multicultural church should be prepared.

A dear Christian friend who works long hours daily with refugees explained to me once a Persian proverb, "He who walks with you over the bridge is your friend until you get to the other side." It means others exist in order to serve your desire to get ahead. From one perspective, this is the direct opposite of Jesus' teaching to go with someone a second mile if they ask you to go one. But actually, this Eastern proverb is hardly different from the Western business mentality about getting ahead at the cost of others!

The point is that there are cultures in which lying is virtually taught as a way of life. When people are used to lying in order to get ahead, their tendency does not change just because they have moved to another land. In fact, at least two pressure points heighten the immigrant's temptation to lie: one, they often come from a shame-culture instead of a guilt-culture. They would prefer to lie about something than to be shamed by it. Secondly, they are starting at the bottom (which can feel shameful). They are at the mercy of their host country and its citizens. To gain papers, acceptance, and work heightens the temptation to evoke sympathy and to create an impression of something that is not true about them. Lying becomes not only a way of life, but a way to improve life in their new surroundings.

This becomes extremely frustrating to the Christian who is pouring out his life for a complete stranger. Many, like my frustrated co-worker above, face the challenge of serving people by listening to their stories but wondering if they can believe them...or worse, the Christian worker trusts them, spends countless hours trying to help them, then finds out the refugee is someone other than what he had described himself to be.

But it is easy to forget that a yet unconverted refugee has little cause to trust you, the Christian worker. He has been taken advantage of for a long time, and especially on his journey through Europe. Why should he suddenly trust you completely? All the more, it is beautiful when after all the trauma, abuse, and deception the refugee has experienced, he does begin to trust you with his true story because he trusts you not to take advantage of him. The most wonderful thing is when the gospel of Jesus begins to so deeply affect the refugee's heart, he makes the decision in any given moment not to lie but to tell the truth. For the Christian worker, this is evidence of a new life springing up in a refugee's heart. It makes all the hard and frustrating hours of service worthwhile.

## Concept of Time

There are other things that create frustration. We in the West have a completely different concept of time than the refugees. Punctuality is not in their way of life and thinking. It is not unusual for a refugee to show up an hour late to his appointment. When he brings his relaxed Eastern way into our tight Western structure of time, it can throw a whole day into disarray. We end up being late to all successive appointments for the rest of the day, while the refugee has no idea how a whole string of people and their families are affected by his not watching the clock to the minute. It takes time for the foreigner to adjust to our way of dealing with time.

New people in our culture require time to learn how to deal with time. For the Christian worker, the slowness, unreliability, and even lethargy of some refugees can be frustrating. To be clear, most of these people were hard-working and successful people in their home country. But once they arrive in the refugee center of a foreign country, there is very little for them to do. Life becomes boring, even meaningless.

## Psychological Breakdowns

In our experience, single men, especially, can fall into a pattern of laziness. They may stay up until early morning hours playing cards, then sleep the day away. Some get into a constant state of lethargy. Others fall into deep depression. All the past tragedy and the current meaninglessness of life create a psychological break-down. The Christian who is trying to serve might think the person is simply lazy, whereas he has actually fallen into a deep, black hole.

We should expect psychological break-downs. If I put myself into the shoes of that young Syrian woman I saw on television this year, a mother of 3 children, who had to watch ISIS soldiers take her husband away to be decapitated, while another soldier grabbed her 2 month old baby by its feet and swung the child's head against the wall, inflicting permanent brain damage, I think that would drive me into deep depression, emotional numbness and a lethargic inability to put one step in front of the other.

Only God can heal these open wounds. As frustrating as the work can become to us, these people need our church communities. They need Christ-centered trauma counseling. They must get to us, and we must have our hearts and doors open for them, prepared with love and trained to take the gospel into their trauma.

## Falling away from Faith

Nothing is as painful as investing yourself for months, even years, in a person's physical comfort, psychological healing and eternal wellbeing, in his months-long preparation for baptism and growth in faith, in challenging his old, destructive patterns and helping him put on new patterns, and giving up so much of your free time, spending sleepless nights, and investing your life into the life of another...and after all that he suddenly falls into some black hole, threatens to kill himself, refuses all help, publicly spews out his hatred toward God for having taken everything he had held dear in his home country, blasphemes God for having replaced his losses with nothing but a faith that brings him nothing, when he yells "so what good is your God!" and tells you to get out of his life because you have done him no good...nothing is as painful as that: it breaks your heart into a thousand pieces.

People can show all the signs of a true conversion, then suddenly throw it all overboard. Some walk away because it is easier to jump into bed with someone than to wait patiently on God for the spouse of God's choice. Others throw their faith away because someone very dear to them died and they attribute the death to an uncaring God. Others get tired of the disciplines and regularity that faithfulness to Jesus and his church require. There are many reasons why people experience "spiritual shipwreck" (1 Timothy 1:19), why their faith is "choked by the cares of the world" (Matthew 13:18-22).

The fact is, that every time it happens to someone in whom you have deeply invested and whom you dearly love, it will rip you apart. Sadly, the more people we lead to the truth of Jesus Christ, the more people there are who will walk away from the truth (2 Timothy 2:18). It pierces our hearts like a knife every time. At such points, we have stepped into the shoes of our Master, who was knifed in the back by Judas, betrayed by Peter, and forsaken by most of his followers in the most important moment of his ministry.

There are enough points of frustration that sometimes we want to throw our ministry to the stranger away. But then, we look again at the people who found help for their living situations with us and ultimately a living relationship with Jesus Christ. Recently a new Iranian was in our worship service. Despite an hour-long train ride, he came the next Sunday and brought seven other Iranians with him. Then he declared for them: "Because of everything that we experienced in Iran and on our journey to Europe, we need love from people and peace with God. We have found both here with your congregation. That's why we'll keep coming back." That is the kind of encounter that can motivate the tired heart of a servant of Jesus.

Completely rewrote this paragraph: It also has a boomerang effect: a German lady had started attending our worship services. After several weeks she revealed to me the reason: "I walked away from God when I was a teenager. There were just so many rules that were preached in my church and I wanted freedom and to experience life on my terms. Now, a husband and two children later, I am disappointed and know I need to make my way back to God. So, I tried your church. I was afraid you might not accept me with all my different ideas and moral failures. But when I saw how this church is so willing and ready to take in people who are as different from mature Christians as Muslims are, I started to believe that things could be good again." That woman has indeed made her way to the cross of Jesus, has experienced God's forgiveness and has had her heart flooded with his peace. My wife, Susan, recently said to me: "All the frustration we have experienced in church ministry was worth it just for her alone!"

To say the least, Pastor Martens has experienced many frustrations and has wept many tears. Besides the tremendous opposition in the neighborhood, he is constantly exhausted from the unending work and long hours. "Working with refugees takes so much time", the man in his late 50s has said. Often, he does not return home until 3:00 in the morning. He speaks of the refugee work as overwhelming: residence status issues, conflict with Muslims in the refugee homes, the need for translation when they have to appear before authorities, the need for German lessons, church asylum, threat of being moved or sent back to their home countries, questions regarding family members that wish to join the person who fled to Germany, and, of course, much counseling for the trauma experienced during their flight.

Martens also sees the connection to Bonhoeffer: „When we view ourselves only as a self-serving corporation, we miss out on something absolutely essential. Or spoken like Bonhoeffer: Church is only then Church, when it exists for others."   And one older member admits, "As the first refugee came, I cried." For her many of these changes are challenging, for example, the long church service, but she says: "Earlier the church service was short, the church was empty, and we were complaining.  Now that hundreds of people are coming, and many Muslims have converted to Jesus, I work hard at remaining thankful and guarding myself against complaining about a three hour service."

## How then Shall We Serve?

The ministry to the stranger brings much frustration with it, but also joy and fulfillment.  What can we do to remain spiritually healthy in such a challenging mission?

- Check your heart daily: you are serving others not for the sake of proving yourself an effective minister of the gospel, nor to have dramatic conversion stories to tell. You are serving others because you love Jesus with all your heart: loving your neighbor as yourself is the way you express your love for Jesus. As you keep your motive focused on your love for Jesus, "do not grow weary in well-doing!" (Galatians 6:9).
- Resist every temptation to grumble, to be negative, to be critical. Jesus is creating atmospheres of harmony and unity. Satan wishes to sow seeds of discord. Stay alert to being positive, patient, and forbearing.
- Spend a significant amount of time every single day in Scripture meditation and prayer. The worker on the front line of battle needs this as daily refreshment and strengthening. Take Luke 10:38-42 as your "posture of preparation": You may like to keep yourself busy in ministry like Martha in the kitchen, but you will not survive the heat of the battle if you do not sit at Jesus' feet in the living room and soak in his presence.
- Make sure you are part of a team of people who are positive, passionate lovers of Jesus, and able to laugh a lot. For all the intensity of ministry you face, you need to surround yourself with people who are positive about life. They need to be mature enough in their faith that they will exhort you to stop whining and complaining, to keep up the disciplines of the soul, and constructively help you to improve your spiritual gifts.
- Be certain you have an army of prayer warriors standing behind you. People need to pray for you daily. They need to be people to whom you can entrust difficult information and who will immediately go to prayer for you. You will fall into many temptations to do wrong, think wrong, react wrong. You need people who in Jesus name can say: "Satan has sought to sift you like wheat. But I have prayed for you" (Luke 22:31).
- Learn how to love those you don't like! You do not have to feel great chemistry with everybody with whom you are working. Especially in a situation in which you have

people of many different backgrounds and habits and ways of communicating, you can work together with people you don't like: you can love a difficult co-worker by showing respect, holding your tongue, being kind and generous, and showing hospitality. Keep your focus on the bigger prize: it's about making Jesus known to those who do not know him, it's not about having warm feelings toward another person. You can love people you do not particularly like.

- Learn to forgive very quickly. You need to take every pain inflicted on you to Jesus and place it into the wounds in his hands. He died on the cross to take the bruises and cuts which you receive in ministry into himself. It is foolishness and a form of unbelief for you to carry in yourself what Jesus took into himself on the cross. Worse, if you do not take your woundedness to Jesus, you will let the root of bitterness grow deeply into your soul and ruin your effectiveness.

### One persons reflections on this:

*Stephen, you are correct. This is so crucial. But let me give the other side, too: We need to teach the refugees how to forgive. This is such a significant part of their spiritual growth, because most of them carry with them the memories of horrible things done to them. Last week in our Persian house church, we had a visitor from England who was a former Iranian Muslim but now a follower of Jesus and a pastor of a small church. At the end of our discussion time, the 13 Iranians and three Americans stood in a circle to close the evening in prayer. The visiting Pastor explained that we were going to pray for forgiveness and restoration. There had been some disagreements and arguments amongst some of them during the past few weeks. The prayer time was powerful, and I was reminded of Paul's writing in 1 Corinthians 12 where Paul teaches on the unity of the body of Christ. Each and every one of the Iranians in the room, most if not all of them former Muslims, prayed for forgiveness for one another. After we finished this prayer, the Iranian pastor asked the three Americans to stand in the middle. They wanted to bless us and ask us for forgiveness. He then explained how in Iran, they were taught since kindergarten, "death to America" and to hate Americans. He had a burden on his heart and wanted to pray for forgiveness on behalf of his people. So, the three of us huddled closely together while the Iranians circled us. As they prayed, it was as if the gates of heaven were opened and the flood of God's love rushed into the room. His presence was so heavy that people, including myself, began to cry. There is power in forgiveness!! Through forgiveness, not only relationships with one another are restored, but the nations are reconciled!*

**Karen Smith, co-worker in pastoral care and refugee ministries**

- Keep preaching to yourself Psalm 53:6. In fact, 366 times the Bible says: „Do not be afraid! " Why? Because in most cases, "there is no need to fear" because God is sovereign and good and sovereign-and-good at the same time!
- Do not fear chaos. Many of us like everything predictable and perfectly organized. People from different cultures bring their languages and mannerisms with them. The more that come, the more your order can be disrupted. Don't worry about it! In many cases, chaos will mean God is doing a new thing! Relax, give your carefully worked out agenda into his hands, and let him do his work!
- Pay attention to your physical and psychological health. The work with people from other cultures, who are often also traumatized, requires so much strength and energy, that you need to have at least one day in the

week for relaxation. The refugees and immigrants need to learn to respect your boundaries. Make it clear to them when you're available and when you're not available. Take extra days off. When you are dedicated to work among refugees on a full-time basis, consider whether after the first couple of years you should switch to another form of work, so that you don't burn out.

- Be careful when you report about God's work in your midst. You definitely want to raise up Christians to pray for you and your church's ministry to refugees. But you must be careful not to needlessly endanger people's lives. Especially when reporting over the internet, such as Facebook, do not show pictures of refugees in connection with you or your church community. Case in point: a Christian was so thrilled about all the Muslims who suddenly appeared in her congregation in Germany, she took a picture of them with her cell phone, then posted it on Facebook. It was a fairly innocent picture, taken from the back of everyone, no faces to be seen. One of the refugees' right jacket sleeve extended into the picture from the left side of the photo. A Muslim in Australia recognized the jacket sleeve as belonging to his cousin. He texted him: "You are a Muslim. What are you doing in a church?" We must protect the lives we serve.

## It's all about Jesus

Never forget, but especially when you are completely exhausted by the work or personally hurt by others: This is all about Jesus and it is all for Jesus! It's not about how successful our ministry can be or what others think about our ministry. Following Jesus is no walk in the park, it is not about how comfortable or easy or fulfilling or pain-free life can be for you. When you are too afraid to take the next step, remember: it is all about Jesus. When you are filled with frustration, anger, or hurt, remember: it is all about Jesus. When the joy is gone, go to the cross, see yourself "crucified with Christ. It is no longer you who lives but Christ who lives in you" (Galatians 2:20).

Early in 2016, I attended a small conference in Europe. Everyone at this conference was serving Jesus in some way somewhere in Europe. The ministry of the previous months and the fast pace I had kept had brought me to the point of exhaustion. I came to the conference tired and in a dark and critical mood. Consequently, when a few people innocently said things to me, I interpreted their words as criticism lodged against my person. I wallowed in their harmless words like my dog used to roll around in mud puddles. By the Sunday morning of that weekend, I felt wounded and angry. I looked for reasons to judge those people who had hurt me, and in my soul, I distanced myself from them and everybody else. The service began with some songs, but I did not sing. One of my close friends prefaced the Lord's Supper by preaching on 'joy'. I felt none of it. My eye brows kept pressing down on me, as I continued to grovel in my pain.

Then an older man, Jim, got up and led us to the Lord's Supper. He started to tell us that the U.S. Supreme Court justice, Antonin Scalia, had recently died. "What does this have to do with Christ's death?" I immediately thought with a critical bent toward my brother in Christ. My thoughts got darker and darker, as Jim went on and on about Scalia having been one of the greatest Supreme Court justices the USA had ever had and that this man would be sorely missed in the Supreme Court. I could not see the sense in these laudatory comments about a Supreme Court judge, when Jim's role was not to lead us into American politics but to the table of the Lord. But Jim continued. He told us how Scalia's funeral was held in a large Roman Catholic cathedral.

Thousands were present, and millions of people watched it on television. The son of Antonin Scalia, a Catholic priest himself, stood to give the homily. Jim read to us what the opening words of the priest's sermon were:

*"We are all gathered here today because of one man. A man known personally to many of us, known only by reputation to even more. A man loved by many, scorned by others, a man known for great controversy and for great compassion. That man, of course, is Jesus of Nazareth "*

In that moment everything stopped for me. All of us were as surprised as the many listeners of the funeral must have been. Jim said to us:

You would expect Scalia's son to talk about his father. But he brought the focus to Jesus, his crucifixion and resurrection. The same is true of us and our circumstances and the ministries we do. You may feel at times like you are dying. That all the air and energy and heart have gone out from you. And you think you deserve a eulogy about all the great things you have done and how you deserve a bit more thanks and respect from others. But the fact is, it's not about you or me. It's all about Jesus!

It hit me deeply: I had been focusing on my pain and how others didn't give me what I thought I deserved and how I deserved a little more respect. But I had placed my life and ministry into the category of MY ministry. I had completely forgotten: "This is not about me! It's all about Jesus! "

As I took the bread and drank the wine, joy returned to my soul.

# EPILOGUE

## October 18, 2017 - Chandigarh, India

I was reluctant when my two colleagues, Vijay and William, urged me to accept the invitation to go to India. "My focus is on Europe and Israel", I retorted. My associate pastor, Vijay Minz, himself from India, responded: "This emphasis on mono-multicultural church, that the base culture of the "monos" needs to initiate open hearts and doors to the other cultures of the "multis", this is precisely what the churches in India need to hear. In fact, I told a pastor in India, who has a lot of influence on other pastors, about what has happened and developed in Frankfurt. He said that with every church being surrounded by Muslims, Hindus, Sikhs, Buddhists, many different castes, and people of all possible nations, they desperately needed to learn to be mosaic churches. He wants to organize a conference and call pastors from all over India, from Nepal, Bangladesh and Buthan together."

"I will pray about it", I offered as a delaying tactic, in the hope that my colleagues would tell me a few days later that Vijay's friend in India had found no interest in Indian pastors and a conference on a strange concept like 'mono-multicultural'.

As I arrived with Vijay at the Chandigarh airport on October 17, I still was reluctant. My reluctance turned to regret in the taxi on the way from the airport to our hotel in the city. Never have I experienced driving in a car like a ski slalom, weaving in and out of everything that moves: on the two-lane highway were three lanes of people either in the direction of traffic or walking across the traffic to the other side, bicycles, rickshaws with children pulled by an older sibling on a bike, carts pulled by humans, slow-moving mopeds, fast-moving motorcycles, buses full of people, cars, bulls and the occasional cow, trucks, and more cars. I have never experienced such chaos. When a day later our driver picked us up from the hotel and drove us to the conference, he asked me: "how do you like driving in India?" I said, "I think it's great. I am ready to die!"

What awaited us at the conference was a complete surprise to me. On the registration table lay T-shirts that had been produced for the over 100 expected pastors. Over the left breast pocket of the shirt the words were imprinted: 'Stand for mono-multi-culture'. I had not even explained the meaning yet, and these pastors were to promote the concept with a T-shirt! The organizer of the conference, Anup Wales, introduced me to a group of pastors who had arrived moments earlier: "Thank you for coming," they said. "We travelled over 2000 kilometers and 40 hours by train to hear about what has happened in Frankfurt." I turned to Anup. "But how can this be? We are 10 little churches, that make up a total of about 450 people. Why would pastors spend so much money and travel so far to hear about such a small happening? God is doing much bigger things on other continents than Europe." Anup smiled. "Pastors are coming from even farther away than these brothers. Some pastors are flying for several hours by plane." I could only shake my head in surprise and amazement.

I began my presentations as I had been asked to do: I told the gathered pastors about the initial vision God had given to me, about the humble beginnings on January 31, 2011 of our seminary student experiment, how we struggled for 19 months but were afraid to quit, about the catalytic moment and developments in October, 2012, the various ways that multiplication happened, how we experienced many God-moments in which it was obvious: we were caught up in a God-orchestrated wave, about amazing conversions the various church plants experienced over the few years (in many cases, just in the last year). I shared with the men and women present, that other churches in Germany and in other parts of Europe were experiencing the same thing with the "invasion" of the refugees.

After speaking intensely in a monologue for 3 hours, I sat down exhausted but thankful to God for the adventure of the past 5 years. Very quietly, Anup asked the pastors to gather in groups of 5-10 people. They should share with each other their response to what they had heard by answering the question: "what does this mean for your church and for churches in India?" Immediately groups formed and lively conversation in Hindi began. After 45 minutes, Anup called on all the groups to report a summary of their answers to the question. What I then heard, destroyed the last remnants of any reluctance I had felt about going to India.

One pastor from a well-known Anglican diocese in India spoke for his group of passion, broken-heartedness, 19 months of persistence and faithfulness to a God-given vision, praise for the seminary students who had started the first church and multiplied it, the American missionary and her impact, then concluded with a plea:

"Brethren, if this is happening in Germany, can it happen in India? We have to catch this vision. Nobody in our group knows how we will do in our cities what they did in the Frankfurt metro region. But a fire has been ignited in our hearts. Let's start these mono-multicultural churches!" The place erupted in applause!

One pastor after another stood and spoke for his group.

"We must repent. We have not taken seriously witnessing the gospel to people of all languages, people groups and nations in our cities."

"We have become legalistic and inflexible, we have become churches for our own kind. The gospel cuts through our self-righteousness and shows us that we are no different than the worst person of any other religion or walk of life. The gospel calls us to love these people, not hate and judge them."

"This is God's time with Germany! He has given that nation a special moment. We pray he gives our country a special time of his Spirit's outpouring."

"Our group was particularly moved by churches being started that are gospel-centered and vision-centered."

"We were struck by these young German students and their humility. How they moved into the lives of strangers, refugees, immigrants with the humble question: 'What may we Germans do for you?' This kind of initiative is God's initiative with us. We must do the same. We must go out of our comfort zones and into the lives of strangers and offer our hearts and lives."

The last pastor to stand and summarize his group's response said the following: "I have attended many conferences, heard many messages and messengers, but this is new. This I hear for the first time. This sounds like revival to the church from God. It has inspired our lives."

This pastor later came to Vijay and me weeping. He asked us to pray over him, that the Spirit of God, who began mosaic churches in Europe, would come upon him, so that he might turn his church into a mosaic church, as well.

I had to think back on the February meeting in the Matthäuskirche in Frankfurt. There also more than a hundred pastors came together, who regretted the past opportunities they had missed, and were united in the decision to now go after the strangers and to integrate people of every language, skin color and nationality in their churches. On that day, February 3, 2016, in Frankfurt, we returned to our churches with the same prayer that we prayed in March in Rotterdam, and then in May in Athens, and now in Chandigarh, India:

"God help us to open our hearts and doors to the immigrants and refugees!" Now is the time!"

# APPENDIX 1

## Recommended resources for mono-multicultural ministry and outreach

**Books:**

Shenk, David W., *Christen begegnen Muslimen: Wege zu echter Freundschaft*, Neufeld Verlag Schwarzenfeld, 2015

Knödler, Matthias/Kowalzik, Thomas/Mulch, Klaus, *Praxisbuch Islam: Wie Christen Muslimen begegnen können*, Christlicher Verlagsgesellschaft mbH. Dillenburg und Orientdienst e.V. Dortmund, 2016

Qureshi, Nabeel, *Seeking Allah, Finding Jesus: A devout Muslim encounters Christianity*, Zondervan, 2014

Mayfield, D.L., *Assimilate or Go Home: Notes from a failed missionary on rediscovering faith*, Harper One,

Richter, Michael, *Fluchtpunkt Europa: unsere humanitäre Verantwortung*, Hamburg: edition Körber Stiftung, 2015

Meinhold, Corinna / Lerz, Anja (Hrsg.), *Warum wir das schaffen müssen: Flüchtlinge – und was wir als Christen damit zu tun haben*, Brendow Verlag, 2016

**Courses & Seminars:**

Al Massira Kurs, www.almassira.org . Contact: international: info@almassira.org ; Deutsch: al-massira.germany@web.de .

## Articles

ReachAcross, Muslimen Begegnen. Schweiz info.ch@reachacross.net .
www.reachacross.ch ; Deutschland: info.de@reachacross.net ;
www.reachacross.de

Arbeitskreis Migration & Integration Deutsche Evangelische Allianz
Orient Dienst, Flüchtlinge Willkommen Heißen: ein Praxisheft für
Christen

Orient Dienst: Orientierung www.orientdienst.de

## Bibles

Persisch-Deutsch: http://medienangebot.ead-
direkt.de/index.php?id=6&tx_mmkbika_pi1%5Btask%5D=item&tx_mmk
bika_pi1%5Bsatzid%5D=2365

Arabisch-Deutsch: http://medienangebot.ead-
direkt.de/index.php?id=6&tx_mmkbika_pi1%5Btask%5D=item&tx_mmk
bika_pi1%5Bsatzid%5D=2390

# APPENDIX 2

## Mission Statement and DNA-Factors of MissionMosaik

**Mission Statement**

MissionMosaik is a movement of churches that recognizes we are living in a special moment in God's mission, and therefore seeks the salvation of all people groups and intercultural reconciliation between nationals, immigrants and refugees through the power of the gospel, in our churches, all across Europe, and beyond.

**The Movement's Core Values**

**Gospel-Driven**

As we submit to the Bible as God's Word and our infallible authority for faith and life, we seek to be theologically robust in our knowledge and proclamation of the Scriptures. The content of the Bible is the gospel, the good news. Through the gospel God saves us. By the gospel Jesus frees us. With the gospel the Holy Spirit fashions us. In all things, we are driven, not by cultural trends or church traditions, but by the gospel.

**Intercultural**

We want to plant new congregations and initiatives and transform existing congregations to be intentionally intercultural. We believe that every church member of the base culture (mono-) is to open his heart, his home and the church community to welcome and serve the people God sends from every language and culture group (multi-). We call for mono-multicultural congregations as the new normal of today's church.

**Missional**

We believe God's Holy Spirit is on a mission to call people of all nationalities and religions to God's salvation through God's Savior, Jesus

Christ. Therefore, we recognize that our country and our immediate surrounding is the mission field of every one of our churches. Our missional focus drives us to much and constant prayer for many conversions and a spiritual awakening of our country in this time. We call on all churches to intentionally structure and strategize their ministries to fulfill our Lord's commission to "go and make disciples of all nations", be they nationals, immigrants or the refugees God has brought to us.

## Multiplicational

As churches who participate with God in his mission, we minister with the mindset that congregations become not necessarily big but necessarily many. Multiplication shall happen with the Mosaik-DNA but in many different ways and forms, in order to impact every corner of society with the gospel. We will train disciples to multiply disciples, leaders to multiply leaders and churches to multiply churches. In this task, we serve and cooperate with all denominations who wish to join us in this intercultural church movement.

# APPENDIX 3

## Worship Resources

**The Lord's Prayer in Many Languages:**
http://www.krassotkin.ru/sites/prayer.su/other/all-languages.html

**The Apostles Creed in Many Languages:**
http://www.knowingjesuschrist.com/the-apostles-creed

# APPENDIX 4

## Footnotes

Estefania Arrazola, Lionel & Naemi Bendobal, Kevin & Chrissy Butzbach, Siggi Dannat, Tirza Eberle, Denis Grams, Stephan Hoch, Sebastian & Judith Kapteina, Thomas Keil, Alena Knauff, Jason Lim, Daniel Lanz, Marie Susann Martel, Albrecht Meinig, Rebekka Peise, Evelyn Reimer, Joel Schäfer, Esther Sidoruk, Kathi Steinhauer, Ben Trakle, Mira Wiessalla, and Thomas Woelki.

[2] On August 3, 1944, less than a year before his death, Dietrich Bonhoeffer wrote from his prison cell in Tegel these poignant words: „The Church is only then Church, when she exists for others" (Bonhoeffer, 6.165). The Lutheran pastor argued that there will always be the church, the "Church for herself", and that she will always be the eminent body of Christ. In actuality, however, the church had stopped functioning the way she should. She had fallen into a rut of stagnation (Ibid., 5.175). Why? Because she was constantly turning around herself (Ibid., 6.164. Bonhoeffer accused even the brothers of the Confessing Church of hiding themselves behind "the faith of the church.") The church is in need of being freed and looking beyond herself. Bonhoeffer suggests that this liberation of the church will only happen when she truly follows Christ: she follows Christ as his body when she does what its head has done. Jesus Christ came into the world for the world. Jesus was God, roughly "existing-here-for-others" (Ibid., 6.163). The church, therefore, only functions as Christ's representative on earth when she exists for others. Bonhoeffer was clear what he meant by "others". God in Christ came alongside the world in order to serve humanity. The church is only Christian, when it goes into the world and serves and saves that which is lost. As long as the church is church-for-the-same she does not fulfill her purpose.

There have been a magnitude of studies done to ascertain exactly what Bonhoeffer had in mind with a "Church for Others". Though Bonhoeffer called for the church of his time to give all it owns to the needy, the hunted and the oppressed of his day, he clearly did not have in mind that the church should amalgamate or dissolve itself into society. Christian Schwark, in Gottesdienste für Kirchendistanzierte, TVG Brockhaus, 2006, p. 74, points to a study done by Scharffenorth, that Bonhoeffer's "Church for others" included mission to people beyond its membership, people estranged from the church. Bonhoeffer was influenced by a famous speech given by Johann Hinrich Wichern in 1848, who spoke of the church as mandated to an "its mission", that God called the church to be the "church for all the people." Wichern's missional appeal had been: "when the people will not come to the church, the church must go to the people". Hans-Arved Willberg's study of Bonhoeffer's ecclesiology (Einer von uns? Willberg, Faix, Gableske, VTR, 2006, pp. 78-119) helped me recognize the relationship between Wichern and Bonhoeffer and the substance of his concept "Church for Others". What impacted my thinking deeply was the claim with which Willberg concluded his analysis: "the continuing work is still waiting to be done. Perhaps as a result of the need, the acknowledgement of the necessity of practice and reflection will come to us again." (p. 119). It matters little of which culture group or nationality we speak, the church is Christ's open door to his own heart for those who are different than the average national. The church-for-others shows a willingness to confront the evils of the world, to speak up for the oppressed, to include people and nationalities that are "other" (Bonhoeffer, 6.163-165).

[3] Examples of concrete core values can be found at https://www.mosaik-nord.de/english/.

[4] This little congregation had actually been planted by Susan and me in 2008, but I turned the leadership over to a graduate of the FTH when in 2010, I suffered a massive heart attack. Bringing this Frankfurt group under our church planting roof and taking its name for all three groups was a sweet rejoining with our former congregation.

[5] Name has been changed.

[6] Name has been changed.

[7] The name and concept come from a ministry to refugees developed by the Evangelical Free Church in Giessen that Karen and the American intern had studied before duplicating it in Frankfurt with the permission of the Giessen brethren.

[8] Names have been changed.

[9] Name has been changed.

[10] From the north (Gießen) to the south of the Rhein-Main area (Darmstadt).

[11] See Timothy Keller and J. Allen Thompson, Redeemer Church Planting Manual, with which we have worked since the beginning.

[12] The pioneers of this system, the City Mentoring Program, are Harald Nikesch, Philipp Bartholomä, Frank Hammann, Norman Tober, Christian Göttemann, Tatjana White, and my wife, Susan. They have worked together for many years,

represent various denominations, and have worked at a high-quality mentoring system for church planting that is now used by many denominations and in several European countries.) See City Mentoring Programm (CMP), http://www.citymentoring.de/ueber-uns/.

[13] See Timothy Keller, Center Church.

[14] Mindy Belz, They Say We Are Infidels: On the Run from ISIS with Persecuted Christians in the Middle East, Tyndale, 2016.

[15] Michael Richter, Fluchtpunkt Europa: Unsere humanitäre Verantwortung, Körber-Stiftung, 2015.

[16] Johannes Reimer, Multikultureller Gemeindebau (city: Franke, 2011, S. 36f.)

[17] You can read more on the theme of the "Theology of the Stranger" in German from Roland Werner, „Der Gott der Flüchtlinge – eine Spurensuche zum Thema Flucht, Flüchtlinge und Heimatsuche in der Bibel", in: Corinna Meinold/Anja Lerz (Hg.), Warum wir das schaffen müssen: Flüchtlinge – und was wir als Christen damit zu tun haben, Moers 2016 (Brendow), pp. 162-167. Cf. Johannes Reimer, Interkultureller Gemeindebau, pp. 32-49.

[8] We see this in Acts 6 in the mono-multicultural make-up of the first diaconal team.

[9] I'm indebted to my friend, Sue Holm, who has become an expert in cross-cultural communication and is often part of our conference team when we talk about the mono-multicultural church as the new normal.

[20] Corinna Meinold / Anja Lerz (Hrsg.), Warum wir das schaffen müssen: Flüchtlinge – und was wir als Christen damit zu tun haben. Brendow, 2016. S. 144-146, my translation.

[21] See Appendix 1 for descriptions and purchasing details.

[22] Tim Hughes.

[23] Two excellent resources for Christ-centred preaching are Brian Chapel…Tim Keller, Preaching…

[24] In the various churches the students and I started since 2011, as described in chapter 1, there is liberty for each congregation to decide what it will teach and practice on the issues of end times, the charismatic movement, and baptism (and to join a denomination that supports its views). On baptism, I personally adhere to the covenantal interpretation: this is not the German Lutheran view, that assigns the new birth to the baptism of infants, but more the English-Scottish

Reformed view, that interprets baptism as the New Testament continuation of circumcision, and, therefore, as the sign and seal of belonging to God's covenant people. Covenant baptism includes both the baptism of new believers as well as the baptism of children of believing parents who are members of the local church community in which their infant is baptized. That is why I like calling the covenantal view of baptism "household baptism", after the 2 baptisms recorded in Acts 16:14-15 and 31-34 and the one mentioned in 1 Corinthians 1:16. It is essentially "new believer's baptism" and that of his offspring, just like Abraham, the covenantal head of the household, was circumcised with all male members of his household, including Ishmael, who God knew would break that covenant and rebel in his heart against the Lord.

[25] Many thanks to Tim Keller for these two core statements of the gospel (Center Church).

[26] According to the Bundeskriminalamt, attacks against refugees and their housing grew to 1027 crimes (of which 173 were violent, 92 were arson), while there were only 199 in 2014 and in 2013 only 69. By October 2016, there were already 800 similar crimes registered; and the number of attempted murders also grew.

[27] See the studies by Allensbacher Institute für Demoskopie "Was ist deutsch?", September 2016, www.ifd-allensbach.de/uploads/tx_reportsndocs/FAZ_September_2016.pdf.

[28] More on this theme can be found, for example, in Herbert Brücker, Auswirkungen der Einwanderung auf Arbeitsmarkt und Sozialstaat: Neue Erkenntnisse und Schlussfolgerungen für die Einwanderungspolitik, Gütersloh 2013; S. 1-6; oder Holger Bonin, Der Beitrag von Ausländern und künftiger Zuwanderung zum deutschen Staatshaushalt 2014, Mannheim 2014.

[29] See information from the Statistischen Bundesamt at www.destatis.de.

[30] Cf. the classic text by Bill Musk, The Unseen Face of Islam, London: Kregel Publications, 2004.

[31] More on the fear of Islam in Attachment A., z.B. Christoph Irion (Hg.), Wer hat Angst vor dem Islam? – Beiträge zu einer aktuellen Debatte, Holzgerlingen 2015 (Hänssler), und Eberhard Troeger, Der Islam und die Gewalt, Gießen 2016 (Brunnen).

[32] See Andreas Baumann, Der Islam – Gottes Ruf zur Umkehr?, Basel: Brunnen, 2003.

[33] Schaffen, p. 160: "Wenn wir uns immer nur als Selbstbespaßungs-Verein ansehen, dann haben wir etwas ganz, ganz Entscheidendes verpasst. Oder, mit Bonhoeffer gesprochen: Kirche ist Kirche für andere".

# ABOUT THE AUTHOR

Dr. STEPHEN BECK (Ph.D.) is the founding pastor of the Mosaikkirche in Frankfurt, Germany. After completing his theological studies in the USA and planting churches in the USA and Canada, he returned to the country of his childhood, Germany, where he serves as Professor of Practical Theology at the Giessen School of Theology (Freie Theologische Hochschule, Giessen). It is from there that he and his wife, Susan, embarked on an astounding church planting multiplication adventure with 24 seminary students, a movement that continues to bring encouragement and hope to Christians and churches even beyond the European continent today. Stephen and Susan have been married to each other since 1976 and have 4 daughters. The couple resides in Frankfurt, Germany.

# Other Titles Available from Greater Europe Mission

## Worth the Risk: What Would You Put on the Line to Share God's Love in Europe?

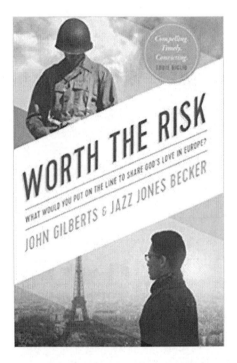

What does it take to be a cross-cultural messenger of the Gospel? This book explores two extraordinary lives that God has used to impact France: Bob Evans, soldier, WWII chaplain, missionary, and founder of Greater Europe Mission, and Jazz Jones, modern-day missionary facing the challenges and trials of ministry in post-modern Europe, including terrorism and religious strife. What was true about the spiritual climate of Europe 75 years ago? What is true today? And what is always true?

Click Here to View on Amazon

# Are You Interested in Experiencing What God is Doing Firsthand?

Consider attending one of our Church Partnership Weekends in Frankfurt, Germany. We usually have two a year.

For more information contact:

Susan.Beck@GEMission.org

21156799R00120

Made in the USA
Lexington, KY
09 December 2018